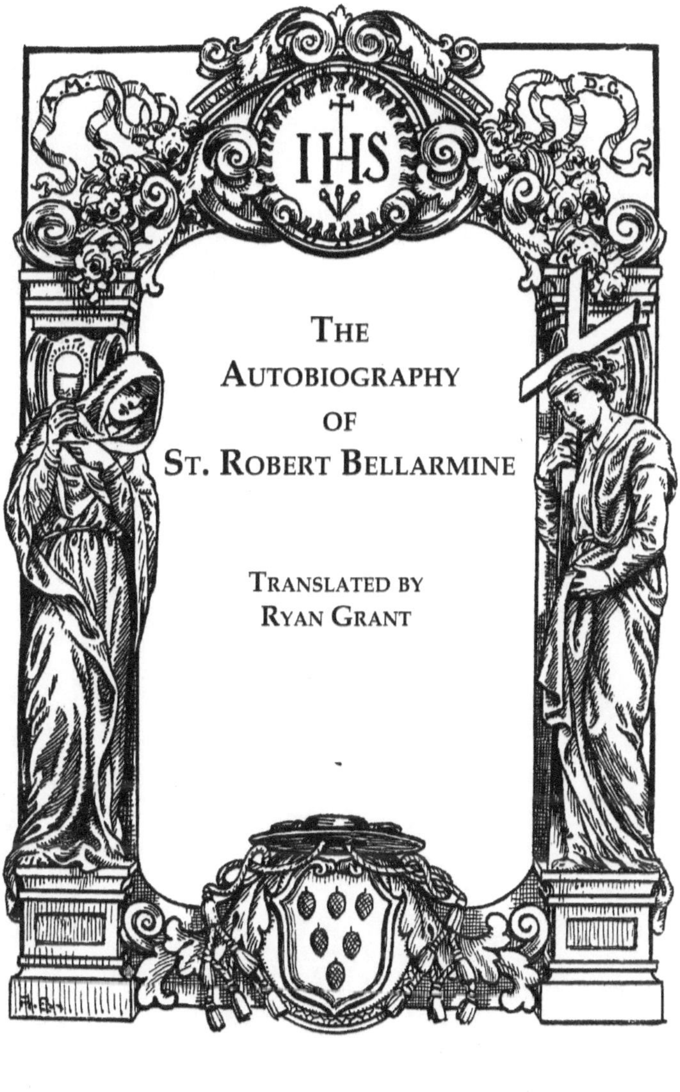

The Autobiography of St. Robert Bellarmine

Translated by
Ryan Grant

The Autobiography of St. Robert Bellarmine

Along with:
The Guide to Composing Sermons
Sermons on the Annunciation

Translated from the Latin by
Ryan Grant

With a Foreword by:
Philip Wolfe, FSSP

MMXVI

ISBN: 978-1-953746-80-1

The Autobiography of St. Robert Bellarmine
Translated from the text provided in Xavier Marie Bachelet, S.J.: *Bellarmine avant su Cardinal.*, pgs. 422-468.

A Guide to Composing Sermons
Translated from *De Ratione Formandae Concionis*
Text in Sebastian Tromp, *Opera Oratoria Posthuma*.

Sermons on the Annunciation
Translated from *Super Missus Est Angelus*
Text in Sebastian Tromp, *Opera Oratoria Posthuma*.

Published by Mediatrix Press
http://www.mediatrixpress.com

©Ryan Grant, 2016

This work may not be reproduced for commercial purposes in either electronic or physical format.

Foreword
©Fr. Philip Wolfe, FSSP, 2016.
All rights reserved.

Cover art: St. Robert Bellarmine teaching Catechism in his titular church of Santa Maria in Via.
Design © Ryan Grant, 2016.

Table of Contents

Foreword. vii

Translator's Preface. xiii

The Autobiography of
    St. Robert Bellarmine. 1

Appendix A
    The Roman College and Scholastic Disputation. 60

Appendix B
    The French Wars of Religion and Henri Bourbon. 64

Appendix C
    St. Robert Bellarmine, Sixtus V and the Vulgate. 71

A Guide to Composing Sermons. 79

Sermons of St. Robert Bellarmine

First *Sermon Super Missus Est*. 87

Second Sermon on the text, *Missus est Angelus*
    97

Another sermon *Missus est Angelus* 105

Third Sermon *Missus est*. 117

Fourth Sermon *Missus est*. 130

Fifth Sermon *Missus est Angelus*. 141

Sixth Sermon on *Missus est Angelus*. 149

Foreword

✠
JMJ

DURING another chaotic time in the Church, St Philip Neri used to tell his directees that he didn't care what they read, as long as the author's name began with the letters "ST." That advice is just as helpful today as it was then, and with his Bellarmine Project, Ryan Grant is making the writings of one such author, the great Doctor of the Church, St. Robert Bellarmine, available to the English speaking public.

This particular book has the added merit of containing the saint's autobiography, (the only account currently in print in English); for that reason alone, it is worth reading. St. Robert himself explains the importance of knowledge of the lives of the saints: "The saints are so many models of virtue and norms of right conduct which God has given us to guide us in our course through life. But again, it is quite impossible to follow another person's example if we do not know who he is or what virtues he practiced and trials he underwent. We cannot imitate an abstract generality. To paraphrase a statement of Christ, the sanctity of the saints is the candle that must not be put under a bushel but upon a candlestick..."[1]

In his autobiography, he gives a perfect example of just such a norm of right conduct, a very sound, practical approach that should be employed by anyone considering a vocation to the priesthood or the religious life, when he tells how he asked a trusted Jesuit friend to speak to him plainly as to how he found life in the Society of Jesus, and whether or not there were any hidden evils or dangers lurking therein. How many disasters could be avoided, how many ruined lives and vocations could be prevented, should everyone pursuing such a vocation follow a similar course of inquiry!

St. Robert tells us that he began preaching years before being ordained, and relates that while he was in preaching in Louvain, "when the sermon was finished, and those present for it went out by different gates, two or three streets were so full that the citizens wondered from where so many men went out; for they said it was several thousands."

And he was truly an extraordinary preacher. His contemporaries reported: "So compelling was the power of his genius that it drew vast crowds

---

[1] *De beatitudine et canonizatione,* cited Fr. John A. Hardon, "Bellarmine's Defence of Canonized Saints", *American Ecclesiastical Review,* Vol. 118, April 1948, pp. 265-273; reprinted on The Real Presence.org.

after him and caused his preaching to bear fruits almost beyond belief."[2]

In that regard, his short work, *The Guide to Composing Sermons*, is of particular interest to me. Given that Christ Our Lord established a Church in which the Faith is spread by hearing, (cf. Romans 10:14-17) having a correct and true understanding of the proper approach to writing sermons should be of paramount concern to anyone charged with the sacred office of preaching. And here we have a saint, famous for his preaching (elsewhere we read that during his time in Louvain, hundreds of Protestants would travel all the way from England simply to hear him preach), explaining just what approach the preacher should take in the writing and delivery of his sermons.

A few excerpts: "many not only preach uselessly, but even with danger to their souls, who propose no scope for themselves." (How often have we suffered through some sermon, and were left wondering: Now what was the point of all that?)

"The purpose of a Christian preacher ought to be to faithfully teach the people that which they ought ... to know about divine doctrine. At the same time, he ought to move them to attain

---

[2] "St. Robert Bellarmine – Preacher" by Fr. John A. Hardon, S.J. *Homiletic and Pastoral Review,* Vol. 47 - #3, December 1947, pp.186-192; reprinted on The Real Presence.org.

virtues and flee vices." "...it is necessary that anyone that is going to preach should, first of all, set before him the scope to which he means to direct his whole action and... he should examine the individual parts of his sermon, and see whether they will bring about the proposed end." (As common sense as all that sounds, how often do we actually hear sermons composed in such a fashion?)

But the work speaks for itself. Read it.
And having read the holy Doctor's advice, you can immediately see how he himself practiced it, by a careful study of the third part of this little work, the seven sermons on the Annunciation. And here too, St. Robert places before us another one of the norms of right conduct, when, in the beginning of his Third Sermon *Missus est*, speaking of St. Gabriel greeting Our Lady by saying *Ave Maria*, he asks: "Why do all preachers begin their sermon with this salutation?"

Why do all preachers begin their sermon by saluting Our Lady with the words of St Gabriel?

Why indeed.
Would that it were true!
A few more comments. In his first sermon, we are treated to a beautiful meditation on the greatness of God. St. Robert's words are very moving - at least to this reader; they're really something to be pondered in a quiet moment of prayer, in front of the Most Blessed Sacrament. I can't believe that this sermon wouldn't stir any

believer in the depths of his soul, and this in spite of the fact that not only are they meant to be heard, and not read, we're also reading them in translation; one can only imagine the powerful effect this would have had in actually hearing the saint preach this sermon himself.

We see his principles applied as we read his sermons. But I don't think that they should simply be read; if we really want to draw forth the fruit they contain, they should be read slowly, prayerfully, meditatively, in a quiet place or before the Tabernacle.

Although any Catholic can certainly draw good fruit from these works of the holy Doctor, I would especially recommend this to preachers, seminarians and deacons who are preparing to preach, or even catechists who share in this mission in a derived way, and I am grateful for Ryan Grant bringing these treasures before a wider audience.

Fr Phil Wolfe FSSP
Feast of St Albert the Great 2016

Translator's Preface

HE *Autobiography* of St. Robert Bellarmine was never meant by the saint to be seen in print. It was written at the request of two Jesuit brothers in 1614 who wished to have an account of his life, and St. Robert set it down as best as he knew how. It is very brief and a very simple account of the events of his time, his memories, and recollections of his achievements (with the help of God), as well as the events that pained him. He can never bear to name himself in the events, so he simply writes in the third person and puts "N." for himself. We never find Bellarmine praising himself, but always others, and those few places where he recalls some great achievement, he either adds a joke to mock himself or else is simply calling to mind an event that took place with God's assistance.

After furnishing it to his brethren, who had asked him for it, the manuscript remained in the Roman College until it was discovered during the 1677 Canonization process. At that time it was produced by the *Advocatus Diabioli*, Bottino, so as to show that St. Robert could not have been a great saint, by taking certain statements he makes there in the most negative interpretation possible. Those advancing Bellarmine's cause carefully vetted it and found it to be in complete conformity with heroic virtue; their arguments were such that Bottini ended his office with the declaration: "Everything I objected against the Venerable Servant of God, on account of my office, seems to have been answered outstandingly."[3] Its appearance in print, however, was entirely due to a different circumstance. In 1714 the famous theologian Prosper Lambertini became the *Advocatus Diaboli*, and was absolutely convinced of St. Robert's sanctity, but the death of the reigning Pope, Clement XI, in 1721 brought the cause to an end. In 1740 Lambertini himself was elected to the Papacy as Pope Benedict XIV. This seemed to be the most opportune occasion ever, except for one thing. Three Cardinals strenuously opposed Bellarmine's beatification and eventual canonization, and the ring-leader was Cardinal Passionei. The official excuse for this was Bellarmine's *Autobiography*, and in spite of the clear vindication, even by the man who first used it to attack Bellarmine's cause, they made this their chief objection. The issues are much wider than our present scope, but we can say that Cardinal Passionei's actual motivation was anti-Jesuit feeling, along with Jansenist leanings, or at least, he was not above using the Jansenists and Gallicans in France and the threat of schism to force the Pope to abandon the cause, while the *Autobiography* was merely an excuse. Pope

---

[3] "... Egregie solutae videantur quae contra Ven. Servum Dei ex munere meo objecti ..." Quoted from the Decree on Miracles, AAS vol. xv, 1923, pp. 234-237.

Benedict XIV sent an interesting letter that bears on this matter:

> 29 August 1753: Our predecessor as Promoter of the Faith, Mgr. Bottini, learned of the existence of the *Autobiography* and desired that it should be produced. In accordance with the duties of his office he passed some criticisms on it, taxing the Servant of God with a species of vainglory, and with having imprudently inserted in the record of his life certain matters that ought to have been kept secret. All these objections were embodied in the *votum* of Cardinal Azzolini, to which the postulators had answered with complete satisfaction, though Cardinal Passionei was not content. Up to that point all was legitimate and above board, but the manuscript life of the Servant of God was afterwards printed secretly at Florence, together with Cardinal Passionei's reflections on it, and the complete work was then made public. ... We do not wish to become involved in this affair, but we have told the General of the Jesuits in confidence that the delay with the cause was *dalle ciarle* of Cardinal Passionei, but to the difficult circumstances of the time, and that we believed that we would render a greater service to his cause and to religion by not wishing to throw oil upon the fire."[4]

---

[4] Quoted in Broderick, *The Life and Writings of Blessed Robert Bellarmine*, vol. 2, pg. 472.

Pope Benedict XIV was even clearer in another letter:

> "With regard to the cause of Cardinal Bellarmine, ... our delay is in no way due to the criticisms of his *Autobiography*, for these had been urged before and were fully refuted and disposed of. As you are well aware the delay is entirely the result of the state of affairs in France."[5]

And that is how Bellarmine's Autobiography came to public attention, strange though it be. Hitherto it had never been published in English. Doing so for the first time serves a two-fold purpose. The first is to supply the average reader with an easy and simple life of St. Robert. What better start could there be than what came from his own hand? There is currently no comprehensive English biography of St. Robert Bellarmine in print. The only two works before now were *The Life and Writings of Blessed Robert Bellarmine*, by James Broderick, S.J., written in 1928, and a redaction by the same author in 1961 titled *Robert Bellarmine, Saint and Scholar*. Both works, even though the latter is half the size, are largely intellectual biographies, so much so that all but the most serious reader will lose heart through the long discourses of political philosophy among other things. In those works, Broderick draws heavily from the work of Fr. Xavier Marie Bachelet, a French Jesuit, who

---

[5] *Ibid.*

labored much to bring the primary source writings of St. Robert out of manuscript into print. It is from Bachelet's work that we take the manuscript that is the basis of this translation.[6]

Thus, we hope to provide a major source of St. Robert's life to lay readers, written in the Saint's own hand, with his anecdotes and honest appraisal of his life. Secondly, we aim to furnish a readable translation of the Autobiography for researchers that do not have the command of Latin, or of Italian, the only other language that it has been translated into. To assist the reader, we have applied information taken mostly from the primary sources furnished to us by the great Fr. Xavier Marie Bachelet, S.J., as well as contemporary historical details from the period. Explanations that were too long for footnotes we have placed in Appendices that can be found at the end of the Autobiography to assist readers with complicated historical events which Bellarmine was in the middle of, and thus were well known to him and the Jesuits he wrote for, but not as much to us today.

Lastly, one thing that stands out in Bellarmine's life is his prolific activities as a preacher; he was perhaps one of the most famous preachers in Italy, and he was long remembered in Louvain where he had preached for 6 of his 7 years there. Preaching was so much of St. Robert's life that he even continued to do this as a Cardinal, something nearly unheard of in Rome at that time. He preached and taught Catechism

---

[6] *Bellarmine avant su Cardinal.*, pgs. 422-468.

in his titular Church of Santa Maria in Via, which can still be found in Rome today off the *Corso*, and it provides much solace from the concourse of noise outside, as if the Saint still looked after it.

Many of his sermons have survived, principally those that he gave in Louvain. They are all in Latin, as they were delivered in Latin to the multi-lingual audience of what was then the Spanish Netherlands and today, Belgium. These are found in Bellarmine's Opera Omnia, and some of these make up the volume *Sermons from the Latins*, which is the only English translation of them apart from his sermons on the *Four Last Things*, which are available in small books from TAN. There is another volume, however, that was just discovered in the 20th century by Fr. Sebastian Tromp, S.J., who found the manuscript of all of the sermons that St. Robert gave in Italy. He brought these into print under the title *Opera Oratoria Posthuma*, and they are published in 9 volumes. This is material that few have seen in English because it was a limited print run at the beginning of World War II, and a select few libraries have them. It is here that I want to especially thank Gonzaga University in Spokane, WA, for the access to these precious volumes which I would not otherwise have had. It is from this volume that we have selected both Bellarmine's Guide to Composing Sermons, and his many Sermons on the Annunciation, to translate them for this book. I plan to do more from this volume in the future.

Lastly, I would like to thank my wife, whose patient assistance and encouragement have made this work possible, as well as the benefactors of the Bellarmine Project.

Ryan Grant
Post Falls, ID
October 2016

Dedicatio

Omnibus benefactoribus laboris S. Roberti Bellarmini votum esse, et praesertim Michaeli Duvallio, praesidio ejus remoto, hic liber fieri non posset.

Dedicated to all the benefactors of the St. Robert Bellarmine project, and most especially Michael Duval, without whose assistance this work would not be possible.

THE AUTOBIOGRAPHY OF ST. ROBERT BELLARMINE

I.

.[1] was born in the year of our Lord, 1542, on the 4th day of October. He had pious parents and his mother was especially so, who was called Cynthia, the sister of Pope Marcellus II. She became acquainted with the Society [of Jesus] through Fr. Paschase Bröet, one of the first ten, who perchance had come to Montepulciano on a journey for the sake of a bath for his sickness. She so honored and esteemed this man that from then on she always loved the Society and desired all of her sons (at that time five) to enter it. She was addicted to almsgiving, prayer and contemplation, along with fasting and castigation of her body.

As a result of these she contracted dropsy and died pious and holy in the year of our Lord 1575, at 49 years of age, or at least around that year. She raised up her sons to piety, and the first

---

[1] Throughout the work, St. Robert refers to himself always in the third person as N. It was written much later in his life for the benefit of two fellow Jesuits. For more on the history and details of this work, see the Translator's Preface.

three (of which N. was the third), she bid to stay together and not mix with other boys, as well as to go to Church every day, which was near to her paternal house, and there to pray before the Blessed Sacrament. She made them accustomed to make their confessions in earnest, hear Mass, and to pray and carry out devotions.

II.

WHILE N. was still a boy, I think of five or six years, he used to speak publicly, and, on a footstool turned upside down, clothed with a string, he began to speak on the Lord's passion. He had no subtle and lofty genius, but was accommodated to all things such that he should be equally adept to take on all disciplines. In youth, he began to love poetry, and consumed a great part of the night in reading Vergil, with whom he had such familiarity that he used no word in his poems that was not Vergilian.

The first poem he wrote was on virginity, and the capital letters rendered it, *Virginitas*. When he was only a youth of 16, he wrote an eclogue on the death of Cardinal De Nobili, which was recited publicly. He wrote at the same time many poems in Latin and in Italian, and especially books which he did not bring to completion because they were obstacles which were strewn before him to prevent him from entering the Society of Jesus. He not only left these books, written in Vergilian style, unfinished but he even burned them because he was ashamed to have written on such matters.

III.

HE wrote many poems at Rome, Florence, in Mondovì, Paris, and then at Ferrara, where he was present to recite a tragic comedy in the presence of the Queen of Spain. Since the man who was prepared to recite a long prologue in excellent style was sick, N. composed, on the spot, a shorter prologue that he could easily call to memory, written in iambic[2] meter.

From such a number of poems nothing remains but a sapphic poem composed in Florence on the Holy Spirit, whose beginning is: *Spiritus celsi dominator axis*, which was commanded into print by I know not whom, without the name of the author, among select poems of illustrious men; and a short hymn on St. Mary Magdalene, which was placed in the Breviary. That hymn was composed in Tusculum, and was chosen in preference to a hymn that Cardinal Antoine wrote on the same saint. Each

---

[2] To write classical poetry well, one had to observe the rules of meter which governed not the rhythm, as we now understand it, but the quantity of vowels and the combinations of long and short vowels. Iambics are classical meter using a *jambus*, which is a metrical "foot" of a short and then long syllable, and in Classical Latin poetry would be used in sequences of 5 feet per line, called pentameter. It is comparatively more difficult than modern poetry. –Translator's note.

of ours were written almost at the same time, but it ought to rather have been held as a joke than to be placed in the Breviary.

IV.

NOW let us return to the time before he entered the Society of Jesus. As a young man of 15 years, as it seems to me, N. gave a sermon or exhortation on Maundy Thursday for the primary Confraternity of the city, which the Prior of the Confraternity usually gave. Although the Fathers of the Society supplied the material, he committed it to memory and applied the words and actions.

Yet, on account of this sermon, he was often compelled by the Prior to speak to the Confraternity, although a short space of time was conceded to him to prepare. In the same time he readily learned to sing easily and play various musical instruments; he also learned to restore nets used for hunting so that it never seemed that they were torn.

V.

IN his sixteenth year, when he was going to journey to Padua for more serious studies, and had already obtained the permission from the Duke Cosimo II of Florence[3] to take up studies outside Pisa, he determined to forget the world and give his name to the Society of Jesus.

It so happened, however, that he thought in earnest on a certain day, on how he could arrive at true peace of soul, and when he had reviewed and pondered for some time the dignities and temporal honors that he could hope to obtain, he began to think in earnest on the brevity of temporal things, no matter how great. Then he conceived a horror of such things, and determined to seek that religious order in which there would be no danger that he would be dragged to such dignities.

Next, knowing that there was no religious order safer in this than the Society of Jesus, he concluded that he must altogether choose this one. He related his desire to Fr. Alphonso Sgariglia, who was then one of his teachers, by whom he knew that he was excessively loved. In confidence as a friend, he asked his faithful friend to tell him without any deceit how he found life in the Society, whether he was content with his vocation, and whether there were some hidden evils or dangers lurking which did not appear openly? For he was afraid that after he entered, he would regret the fact. The good Father said that it was the best and he lived very contented.

At the same time, Ricciardi Cervini, his cousin, announced his vocation to the Society of

---

[3] Montepulciano was within the political control of Florence, and in those days it was necessary to obtain permission from your sovereign to travel abroad. –Translator's note.

Jesus. Such a vocation seemed to coincide at the same time. So then, he was quite confirmed, and in turn, after he had given and received letters, he sought from the Reverend Father Laynez, who then was the Vicar General, to admit him to the Society. Yet, because his father wanted him to remain for a year for the sake of his parents, both N. and Ricardo's parents asked from the Reverend Fr. Laynez, that they would remain for a year to prove the spirits.

The Father General conceded, and said this year would serve for proving the two cousins.[4]

VI.

HEREFORE, they both remained at home for part of 1559 and part of 1560, together in a country called *Vivo*, without any interference from their parents. In that time they devoted themselves to frequenting the sacraments and to humanist studies.

Daily, after table they made an Academy, and Lord Alexander Ricciardi, the father, taught something from the *Georgics* of Vergil. Furthermore Ricciardi himself explained Aristotle's Greek *Poetica;* his brother, Herennius (who later died as a Protonotary and

---

[4] According to correspondence, as the next paragraph makes clear, Fr. Laynez counted this year as the novitiate, which would be highly irregular by the later constitutions, but was acceptable in those times if the good life and learning of the candidate was known. –Translator's note.

Referendarius of each Signatura), explained Demosthenes' oration for the crown, and N. explained the oration, *pro Milone* [of Cicero]. Also, they explained Christian Doctrine in the Church, and exhorted the country folk, but not frequently.

After a year had gone by they took leave of their parents and came to Rome, and were admitted to the Society on the vigil of St. Matthew in 1560. After ten days of the first probation, in which they boarded as guests, they were admitted to the common association. Then after serving the cook seven days and in the refectory for seven other days, they so satisfied the novitiate, that they were sent to the College. On the feast of the Circumcision they renewed their vows, which they had made of their own will, on the first day of their entrance, with the other members of the order.

VII.[5]

N. remained in the Roman College for three years studying Logic and Philosophy under Fr. Pietro Parra, and although he was sick for the whole three years (from the first year he labored under a serious lethargy, in the same and following year he labored with continuous headache, and in the third was judged tubercles and near death), still, he defended the first monthly conclusions, and at

---

[5] For more on the nature of studies and the Roman College, see Appendix A.

the end of the course he defended all of philosophy.

Although there were ten or twelve fellow students who were made masters, he alone answered all the questions on the soul, and without a president he defended against the master's arguments. He did not remember whether they were one or many, and the day before his day he was sent to the vineyard with some companions to distract him from study and commentary, lest his weak health would become worse.

VIII.

N the year 1563 he was sent to Florence to teach humanities. There, through the change of air and a cure from a very good doctor, he began to be in much better health. He taught youth in the schools as best as he could, by mixing in philosophical questions to prove his authority.

In the summer he also taught astronomy with a treatise *de stellis fixis*. In his primary residence he gave two Latin orations, and wrote hymns for the great feasts, which he fastened to the doors of the Church. As winter rolled in he began to preach on Sundays and feasts after Vespers at his superior's command, although he was only 22 years old, beardless, and without any orders, nay more without the first tonsure.[6]

During the first sermon a certain pious woman always remained praying on her knees; when she was questioned about this, why she did so, she answered that, when she saw a beardless youth in the pulpit, she feared lest he would altogether lose heart and so disgrace the Society. But N. then acted with a greater spirit and boldness than he would later as an old man, for his memory then seemed to be solid. He also began to give exhortations to his brethren at home by his superior's command.

IX.

HEN N. was at Florence in the fall he traveled with Fr. Marco to Camaldoli, Mount Avernia and Vallombrosa, and on the journey he preached to the country folk and the townsmen while Fr. Marco heard the confessions.

At Camaldoli he was received very kindly by the *Major* (as they call the General) and for three days he tarried there. On the third day the *Major* commanded N. to give an exhortation to the Fathers of that place, though he was altogether unprepared; he did so unwillingly and coerced, but the venerable old men listened attentively,

---

[6] At this time the Council of Trent was still coming to completion, and the practice of licensing preachers who were not yet in orders was still in vogue. Such a thing is forbidden today by the Code of Canon Law.

and then wished to kiss N's hands, which was overwhelming for a young man, so he would not suffer it to be done.

Still, he only remained in Florence for a year and a month. Then he was sent to Mondovì, or Mons Regalis; he had one companion from the brothers all the way to the sea, and a little beyond Lucca. Next, he sailed alone to Genoa, then Savoy, and thence arrived from his journey to Mondovì.

On that journey he endured many dangers of body and soul. For example, in a certain inn, the innkeeper's wife said he was the long absent husband of her daughter, in another a certain man said that N. stole his purse at night. But God came to the assistance of the innocent man and he firmly determined that, if he was ever in a position of authority in some house of the Society, he would never send the Fathers or brothers alone, especially youths, even if it would be a great expense.

X.

N the college of Mondovì he discovered in the catalogue of lessons for that year that he was assigned to teach Demosthenes the Greek orator as well as Cicero and certain others. Since he hardly knew Greek, apart from the alphabet, he said to the students that he wished to instruct them from the foundations [of Greek], first teaching them grammar, then Demosthenes.

Therefore, daily he learned what he was going to teach them with the greatest effort he could muster; at length, he so completed this burden that in short order he could explain Isocrates and then other books.

In the summer he taught the *Somnium Scipionis*, explaining many philosophical and astrological questions, and many came to listen, even from the Doctors of the University who then resided there.

On the feast of Pentecost he preached for three days being practically forced against his will, and although he was unworthy, it was written by the superior to the Roman Fathers that a man never spoke as this man. He continued to preach on Sundays for nearly three years, the whole time he was there, especially in Advent and the feasts of Christmas.

XI.

T happened to him by chance that he read the sermons of the Bishop Cornelio di Bitonto, and began to write sermons in imitation of his style, and recite them (not without great labor); however, on a certain day of Christmas he gave a very elaborate sermon after vespers, which he had consumed several days in memorizing; the Canons of the Cathedral gave a sign that they wanted him to give a sermon on the following day in the morning. Therefore, N. nearly despaired. How could he preach when he did not even have one

hour to commit the sermon to memory? But it pleased God that N. never preached with so much fruit and so freely as when he did so from his heart. For the Canons said: "Previously, it was you that preached, but today, an angel from heaven preached." From that time he determined to altogether cast off the ornamentation of words, and only write points in Latin, which he did even in his Latin sermons.

XII.

IN that college at Mondovì, N. nearly always exercised offices; he taught in schools, read at table, preached in Church, held exhortations for the brothers, accompanied the priests to their business, helped the porter, and when he ate, he also, at some time in the morning, woke up those who were asleep. But when Fr. Adorno, the Provincial, heard him preaching, he said it was not good that N. should delay theological studies for so long, and commanded him thence to set out for Padua, that after taking a theological course, he should free himself for preaching alone.

Before he left Mondovì, or Mons Regalis, a humorous incident happened to him. He was a companion of Fr. Rector to visit the Dominicans. The Prior of the Dominicans invited the Rector to drink, and when he agreed, the Prior said about N., whom he did not know: "Well, your companion, this little brother here, will be glad of a drink."[7] The next day, that Prior came to the college and found N. carrying out the duty of the porter at the gate, and asked him to call the preacher. N. responded that the preacher could not come, but he would faithfully relate what message his Paternity would entrust. "No," said the Prior, "I cannot tell you what I want, but take me to the preacher, or call him to me." "I already said," N. replied, "The preacher will not come," and when the Prior insisted, N. was compelled to say, "I am whom you seek, and I cannot come, because I am here." Then the prior blushed to remember the impertinent joke of the previous day, and humbly begged forgiveness, and asked if N. would preach on Christmas, when he would publish a Papal Bull containing indulgences for almsgiving, made for the support of the general chapter of the Dominicans that was going to be held, which N. promised he would do, and did.

XIII.

N 1567, N. came to Padua and began his theological studies. Then, two of our brethren had teachers, one of the house, who was Fr. Carolo Pharao, a Sicilian, who taught the *Pars Prima* of [the *Summa Theologiae*] St. Thomas, the other in the public schools, Fr. Ambrose Barbaciarium, a Dominican, who taught the treatise *De Legibus* from the *Prima Secundae* of St. Thomas. But because our brothers and N. noticed that Fr. Ambrose said nothing except

---

[7] *Bebera bene questo fratino vostro compano.*

what was found in Domingo de Soto's book, *De Justitia et Jure*, we quickly took our leave of him, and when Fr. Carolo taught predestination from foreseen works, N. placed the opinion of St. Augustine on gratuitous predestination in his writings.

But scarcely had two months of theological study gone by when N. was compelled to preach in the Church of the college, first before lunch, then after lunch.

During carnival he set out for Venice, and there gave a sermon on the Thursday of Carnival in a gathering of many noblemen, where he was attentively heard arguing against dances and other insanities of that time. When he finished, many of the nobles of the senate wished to kiss his hand.

XIV.

N the month of May, N. was lead to Genoa by Father Provincial on the occasion of a provincial congregation to defend conclusions and preach. Therefore, he withstood conclusions for two days in the Cathedral Church, from the Rhetoric of Aristotle, from Logic, the Physics, Metaphysics, Mathematics and from all parts [of the *Summa*] of St. Thomas.

During the disputation, when he did not agree with his president, Fr. Carolo Pharao, Father Provincial commanded Fr. Carolo to be silent and permit N. to respond by himself. He also gave a sermon on Sunday after Vespers in a very great crowd of listeners, but took nearly the whole discourse from St. Basil on the verse, *Attend to Yourself,* for he knew in that auditorium there were not many who would recognize the theft from St. Basil.

XV.

FTER another year passed by, N. was commanded by Fr. General to set out for Louvain to preach Latin sermons, and there complete the course of theological studies; but because he had begun at Padua an explanation of the psalm, *Qui habitat,*[8] from the pulpit, and was avidly listened to, the Paduan Fathers refused to send him, and they intervened with Fr. General, saying that it was dangerous, N. could not pass through the German cold in the winter, and this is also the judgment of the doctor.

On the other hand, N. wrote to Fr. General that he was ready to set out immediately and in obedience to whatever he would command. At any rate, he did not set out, because his Paternity did not command him to go; rather he commanded his immediate superior to send him. Fr. General waited six months, in which time N. heard Fr. Joannes Ricasolus teaching some questions of the *Pars Tertia* of St. Thomas, and continued his readings on feast days in the

---

[8] *Psalm 91 (90).*

Church on the Psalm, *Qui habitat*, and gave exhortations to the brethren on Friday.

XVI.

HEN the year 1569 began, Fr. General wrote to N. that he should set out for Milan and there join himself to Fr. Giacomo Flandro, then to go to Louvain from there. Since the journey was said to be exceedingly dangerous because of the soldiers of the Duke of Zwei-Brucken,[9] who passed from Germany into France by that route which we were going to take, N. consigned himself to the Blessed Sacrament and there offered his life to God with his whole heart, disposing himself for whatever would happen to him on that journey.

Then, filled with great confidence, he went without a companion to Milan, where he joined with Fr. Giacomo and his Lordship William Allen, who later was a Cardinal, along with two other Englishmen and one Irishman, and they set out for Louvain. When he arrived at the college he said, "I am sent by Fr. General to remain here for two years, but I will be here for seven." And it so came to pass. By what spirit he was lead to say this, I do not know, except that it so came to mind.

---

[9] Wolfgang, the Duke of Zwei-Brucken, who was a Protestant. –Translator's note.

XVII.

E began to preach in Latin on the feast day of St. James the Apostle; since it seemed improper that he still had no ecclesiastical orders, and could not wear a stole, as all preachers there usually did, the Fathers of Louvain wrote to Fr. General on this matter. He deferred the ordination, lest N. be compelled to discharge the profession of the three vows according to the decree of Pope Pius V, but then he wrote back that N. should make the profession of the three vows, and so be ordained, and later would make the profession of the fourth vow.

Due to the fact that there was neither a Bishop at Louvain nor any neighboring places, he was compelled to set out for Liège, where he received the first tonsure on the ember days of Lent, and the four minor orders as well as the subdiaconate. Then he set out for Ghent, and received the diaconate from Cornelius Jansen on the Saturday, *Sitientes*,[10] and the priesthood on Holy Saturday, and during the octave of Easter solemnly sang his first Mass at Louvain with a deacon and subdeacon, in the year 1570.

---

[10] Passion Sunday, that is the 5th Sunday of Lent.

Montepulciano

Cardinal Roberto de Nobili was a youth from Montepulciano and nearly contemporaneous with St. Robert Bellarmine. He was fluent in Latin and Greek at age 12, and became one of the famous figures of the city.

Paschase Bröet

An early companion of St. Ignatius of Loyola, who gave a spiritual conference to St. Robert's mother convincing her that her sons should be Jesuits.

Diego Laynez

One of the first companions of St. Ignatius and the first superior general of the Order after Ignatius' death.

THE ROMAN COLLEGE
The Roman College as it was in St. Robert's time. It was the first Jesuit university and the predecessor to the Pontifical Gregorium University, constructed by Pope Gregory XIII.

MONDOVÍ

The University of Louvain as it was in Bellarmine's time.

XVIII.

N the same year, at the beginning of October, N. was asked by the Fathers to teach scholastic theology. He agreed and although he had not heard some of the *Prima* and *Tertia Pars* [of the Summa], nevertheless, placing himself before the Lord, he taught the whole *Prima Pars* in two years; then part of the *Prima Secundae* in one year; the *Secunda Secundae* in two years; then the beginning of the *Tertia Partis* in another year.[11]

Furthermore, he preached the first six years, and in the seventh ceased from preaching since his strength had been broken; and he taught the last six years. Hence, he preached only in the first year, and the last he only taught, and in the five intervening years he did both at the same time. He was neither free from giving exhortations at home, nor from hearing confessions.

---

[11] What Bellarmine says here is actually significant but will be lost on modern readers without some explanation. The course of studies in Theology at that time began with the Sentences of Peter Lombard, which was a tried and true method going back hundreds of years. Bellarmine had only a few years of studying Theology and had not even taken his doctorate in it, but had taught himself with the aid of the Angelic Doctor. He had told his students, while giving great respect to Peter Lombard, that they would make far more progress with the *Summa*. His departure from the traditional system was actually a radical step, but one that bore tremendous fruit. –Translator's note.

N. was the first to open the theological school of Louvain for all the students, for up to that point the University had not permitted us [the Jesuits] to teach publicly. And because Michael du Bay (Baius), an otherwise distinguished doctor, followed many opinions which seemed to lean to the new errors of the Lutherans, each were condemned by Pope Pius V in the year 1570. N. seeing that many, whom these opinions pleased, did not cease to hold them, began to refute them not as the teachings of Dr. Michael, but as the teachings of the old and new heretics.

XIX.

IN that time, N., thinking that the Hebrew language would be extremely useful for the understanding of Sacred Scripture, applied his mind to learn it, and when he learned the alphabet from someone that was an expert in that language as well as some rudiments of grammar, he made for himself a Hebrew grammar, by an easier method than the customary books of the Rabbis.[12] In short order it seemed he knew

---

[12] In our day we have grammars and courses of Hebrew, but in Bellarmine's day there were no such resources. The main book was the "Rules of the Rabbis" and several others like it, which were disjointed commentaries drawing from different sources from which one could draw grammar and vocabulary. Bellarmine published the very first Hebrew Grammar, *Institutiones Linguae Hebraicae* which became the standard work for two centuries.

enough of the Hebrew language as was sufficient for a theologian.

He then established an Academy in which he might exercise the study of Hebrew and Greek with several others. That he might show his grammar was easier than the rest, he promised one of his students in the theological school, who was altogether untrained in the Hebrew language, that he would so effect that, in the space of eight days, if he meant to apply himself to it, he would learn sufficient Hebrew that, with only the aid of a dictionary, he could understand the Hebrew books himself.

He so applied himself, that he showed he did not think it false, what St. Jerome wrote about Blesilla, that he learned the Hebrew language not in a few months, but days.

XX.

I N 1572, during the Octave of the Apostles, N. made his profession of the fourth vow.

In that same year many cities defected from King Philip, and when the Prince of Orange came with a great army against Louvain, nearly all the religious left because the city could not be easily defended, and the Calvinist heretics, who filled the rank and file of the Prince's army, were particularly savage against religious.

Yet, because the enemy was much nearer than was hoped, the Rector of the College bid

---
–Translator's note.

everyone to change their clothing as well as to cut their hair so that the clerical crown would not be visible, and he divided a small amount of money between those who were at the college, sending them two by two to save them from the imminent danger in whatever way they could.

Then N., with one companion, left on foot towards Artois, for many days and with great labor and danger, until he came to Douay, where, fleeing war, he discovered that plague was ravaging the city. But God delivered them from all dangers.

XXI.

NETIME it happened that, with night threatening, N. was so tired that he could not in any way continue. Therefore, it was necessary that he hold to the road, an exceedingly perilous road; yet behold, a carriage running up quickly, full of men and fleeing the face of the enemy, approached and, since the coachman understood that N. could not continue any further, he stopped and gladly received him into the coach, while his companion ran ahead with stronger feet, until he came to the suburbs of the city.

That coachman was a good man, and a good Catholic. He said that he used to hear Mass daily, but now he made himself hear two Masses daily in hatred of the heretics, and said for that reason he would gladly take N. into his coach, because he had heard from his companion that N. was a priest even though he was wearing layman's garb.

XXII.

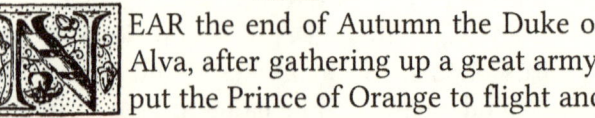EAR the end of Autumn the Duke of Alva, after gathering up a great army, put the Prince of Orange to flight and recovered the cities lost in Hainaut and Brabant, and then N. returned to Louvain to the pristine office of preaching and teaching.

How large the crowd of listeners was can be gathered from the fact that when the sermon was finished, and those present for it went out by different gates, two or three streets were so full that the citizens wondered from where so many men went out; for they said it was several thousands.

When N. went to give a sermon on a certain day (for the college was sufficiently far away from the Church of St. Michael, where he gave the sermon), a certain important man joined him, but he did not recognize N. was the preacher, because he was of short stature and always seemed tall in the pulpit on account of a stool that he stood on. Now, the word had gone out through the town that a giant youth from Italy came to give Latin sermons; he began to ask many questions of N., whether he knew the preacher, why he was there and where he studied, and at the same time to praise him more than was true; but when N. responded, so as to not make clear who he was, the man said, "You are going much too slow and, begging your forgiveness, I desire to run along and find a place." N. replied, "Do as you please, for a place will not fail me."

XXIII.

N the fruit of the sermons, I can say this alone. In a certain sermon given on death on the day of All Souls [November 2], a great movement to penance was aroused; the same thing happened in a sermon given on the Sunday within the Octave of Corpus Christi; many were confirmed in faith in the truth of the Lord's body in the Eucharist, as well as converted from error, as I had received it on the authority of trustworthy men.

Now, many other things were said, on account of which the Fathers of the Louvain College would not submit to N. leaving, although he was urgently asked for by Cardinal Borromeo, who is now called Saint Charles, and he had been promised to him by Father General; in like manner, he had been asked for by the Parisian Fathers. But in 1576, since it seemed his health was so broken that in the judgment of the doctors they could no longer impede his removal without a grave scruple of conscience, so that he could have a change of air, then the General wrote for them to immediately send him to Rome, which they also did.

XXIV.

AFTER N. descended from Aosta and began to take in the Italian air, it was a marvel how he sensed the change in his body. His strength seemed to return and he got better from various sufferings with which he was afflicted.

Therefore, he arrived at Rome exceedingly confirmed, such that after one or another month, he began, at the command of his superiors, to explain the controversies in the Roman Gymnasium, in which office he persevered for eleven years; meanwhile, with the exhortations he gave in the college, he freed himself to hear the confessions of the brethren of the society.

In 1584, unless I am mistaken, N. began to write and publish books, and his first book to be published was his *Institution of the Hebrew Language*. Then there were three books on the *Translation of the Roman Empire* against Illyricus;[13] later he published the first volume of the Controversies, which afterward was divided into two on account of its great size;[14] then he

---

[13] Illyricus is the Latin *nomme de plume* for Mathias Francowitz, one of Luther's most energetic disciples whom Bellarmine often wrote against on historical matters. –Translator's note.

[14] In the first edition at Ingolstadt, the first volume embraced Scripture, Christ, the Papacy, the Church (Councils, the Church Militant and Marks of the Church), Clergy, Monks, Laity, Purgatory, relics and canonizations. The printers at Paris in 1614 broke it up after the work of the Papacy, putting all the rest in a

published the second volume, which later was called the third. At the same time, he published several other books in which are contained minor works.

XXV.

IN 1589, when Cardinal Cajetan was sent as a legate into France on account of the most serious convulsions of that kingdom, N. was sent with him by Pope Sixtus V.[15] In France N.'s name began to be famous on account of the books of the controversies that had been published; therefore many desired to see him and frequently visited him. On the journey, the Illustrious Legate asked of N. how long he thought the Pope would live; he responded that he would die that very year, and often confirmed it at Paris, while the Cardinal altogether declared he was going to live longer.

When the Cardinal Legate and his company were at Dijon, and thought to leave there so as to set out for Paris, a rumor went out that, in a certain fork in the road, the Lord Tavines lay in ambush with a thousand knights to take the Cardinal and kill some of his entourage while capturing others; another went out at the same time that this was a ruse to put a halt to the Cardinal's progress.

---

smaller volume. –Translator's note.

[15] For more on the history and reasons why Sixtus V sent this legation to France, see Appendix B.

As a result, since the Cardinal could not know the truth by human means, after the celebration of the Mass, when all were prepared for the journey, he had secretly placed in the chalice two little pieces of paper; on one of these it had been written *go*, on the other, *don't go*, and commending the whole business to God, he chose his lot, which read *do not go*, and a little later it was made known to him that what was said about the ambush was true.

XXVI.

WE remained at Paris from 20 January even to the beginning of September; for all that time we did nearly nothing, but suffered many things. For when the Duke of Mayenne clashed with the King of Navarre on 12 March, and the King was victorious, a fear and tremor fell upon us. But the King, refusing to destroy and despoil so great a city, preferred to take it by siege than invade it by force. Therefore, he surrounded the city and we all spent our time miserably and destitute of provisions; for broth cooked in a jar with dog meat was sold especially dear.

The Spanish Ambassador gave to us for a great gift part of his horse which he had killed for food. There, N. did nothing except that in the name of the Cardinal Legate, he wrote a letter in Latin to the Bishops of France, dissuading them from schism, because it was related that some of them meant to compel a national Council and in it to create a Patriarchy independent from the Apostolic See, but this was stopped.

XXVII.

IT happened in the month of September, that a letter was conveyed to the Cardinal from Rome; how it made it through is a wonder since the city was closed off on every side; and some speculated certain things about this letter, before the Cardinal opened it, that it forebode bad news, because Pope Sixtus had become hostile to his Cardinal and the secretary, and even to Bellarmine himself on account of a proposition found in his books denying that the Pope is directly the master of the whole world; then N. said that in this letter an announcement of the death of Sixtus V was contained. And everyone laughed at him, because they had heard nothing of any illness of Sixtus. Nevertheless what N. affirmed was true, and they all marveled.

XXVIII.

RETURNING to Rome, N. fell very ill at Meaux. That city was then being ravaged by a deadly form of dysentery, which almost invariably made an end of its victims. N. caught this disease the very first night of our stay, and was also stricken with a most dreadful fever, so that he could neither eat anything nor get a moment of rest. The Cardinal delayed his departure for a day, and then, while consulting with his suite as to what had best be done with N. God put the kindly thought into his heart not to leave him there, but to take him along by some means or other. So he had a litter made ready, and directed that N. should be hoisted onto it. By the goodness of God, as soon as they left the city N. began to get better, and at the end of eight days, during which time N. made the journey sometimes lying down and sometimes sitting up in the litter, at last he was completely restored to health. On the journey he passed through Basel but was not recognized; after it was heard that N. was there, they relate that many were very sad that they could not have seen him; whether they meant to do him harm or honor him is uncertain.[16] He arrived at Rome on the eleventh of November.

XXIX.[17]

IN 1591, when Gregory XIV pondered what needed to be done about the Bible edited by Sixtus V, in which many things were inadvisably changed, and serious men were not lacking who thought that it should be publicly forbidden, N., in the presence of the Pope, showed that this Bible should not be forbidden, but so corrected that, for the sake of

---

[16] Basel was a Protestant city. –Translator's note.

[17] For more information on these issues, see Appendix C.

the honor of Pope Sixtus, the Bible in question could proceed after it was emended.

What should be done, then, was that the inadvisable changes should be abolished as quickly as possible, and the Bible reprinted under the name of the same Sixtus, with a preface added to it wherein it would be shown that in the first edition of Sixtus, due to haste, some errors crept in whether of the printers or of other persons. And so N. rendered to Pope Sixtus good for evil. For Sixtus, on account of that proposition on the direct rule of the Pope over the whole world, had placed his controversies on the Index of forbidden books until it would be corrected; yet, as soon as he died, the congregation of Sacred Rites immediately commanded his name to be erased from the book of the Index.

N.'s counsel pleased Pope Gregory, and he commanded that a congregation be made to revise the Sixtine Bible quickly, and made uniform with the ordinary Bible, especially that of Louvain. That was done at Zagarolo, in the house of Cardinal Mark Anthony Colonna, with Cardinal Colonna himself present, Cardinal Allen of England, and also the Master of the Sacred Palace, with N. himself and three or four others; and after the death of Gregory and Innocent IX, Clement VIII published the revised Bible under the name of Sixtus with a preface, which N. composed.

XXX.

IN fall of 1591, N. withdrew to Tusculum to write the third volume of the Controversies, which he completed and published in a few months, and dedicated to Clement VIII. In 1592, N. became the Rector of the Roman College, and that he might offer an example of religious simplicity to others, he took from the office of the Rector various precious furniture and commanded they be placed in the Sacristy to preserve the vestments and other sacred things; likewise, he also removed some paintings, with beautiful frames, which were not necessary, and only wished to have those things which the other brothers had.

He did not finish his three years, but was sent to Naples to be the Provincial there, and he tried in such a duty to teach others by word and example as well as visit the province twice.

XXXI.

NEVERTHELESS, he did not finish three years, for after the death of Cardinal Toledo, he was called to Rome by Pope Clement VIII in 1597, in the month of January, and the Pope willed to call him into the palace that he might abide there; but he obtained through Cardinal Aldobrandini that he would reside in the [Apostolic] Penitentiary rather than in the palace, and at the same time was made a consultor of the Holy Office.

In that time the Pope began to send him pleas for matrimonial dispensation and several other things. Still, he very rarely, and only with the greatest necessity, went to the palace. In regard to Pope Clement something wonderful happened. For in the first year of the pontificate, when many suspected that he was going to die soon, like his three predecessors, N. said to Sylvius Antonianus that Clement VIII will live for twelve years; he often repeated this, and in the last year he often said to his household that in that year the Pope was going to die.

Though he was neither an Astrologer nor a Prophet, he still so spoke in that case. Then at the request of Cardinal Taurusio, he wrote a short Catechism, as well as a larger one, which a little later were printed, and are found in many places.

XXXII.

N 1598, the Pope set out for Ferrara, and took N. with him; he not only exercised the office of consultor of the Holy Office, but even of examiner of future Bishops,[18] and treated the business of the Society with the Pope, which was demanded on the part of the General. Although N. abided in the college of the Society, still, the Pope gave 25 scudi to the college for each week of his stay.

---

[18] It was in this capacity that St. Robert became friends with St. Francis de Sales. –Translator's note.

XXXIII.

N the year 1599, on the Ember Wednesday of Lent, the Pope created N. a Cardinal so unexpectedly that N. did not even see it coming.

Still, because many had suspected it, Fr. General asked the Pope two months earlier through the Chamberlain whether it would please him that N. be made Rector of the Penitentiary, and with the Pope's agreement, he was made the rector of the Penitentiary. But the Pope permitted this to hide his real intent, just as he also did when, before the mid-year at Ferrara, a member of his household said that N. is worthy of the Cardinalate, and the Pope responded: "Indeed he is worthy, but he is a Jesuit," hinting that he would not do it.

Therefore, when it was announced later in the consistory that N. would be a Cardinal with twelve others, on the spot he sent Cardinal Aldobrandini, the Marquis of Sanesio to N. who showed him that he would be made a Cardinal and commanded him in the name of his Holiness to not leave the house in any manner. Then N. called all the fathers of the Penitentiary to himself and asked for counsel, namely what he ought to do. Fr. John Baptist Costa, who was the eldest of all, said there was no place for consultation, because when he was made a Cardinal and it was declared in consistory, there was no hope that the Pope would accept any excuses, especially when he had expressly commanded that he should not leave the house.

The others said the same thing. Then N. sent Fr. Ministro to Cardinal Aldobrandini, who said to him that N. desired to go to the Pope to explain his reasons why he could not accept this dignity, but he did not dare to leave the house on account of the prohibition made in the very name of the Pope. Cardinal Aldobrandini responded that he could not concede that N. should go to the Pope except when called, because the Pope did not wish to hear him, but commanded that he accept this dignity from obedience.

Later, he was called to receive the hat, that is the red biretta, and wishing to begin his excuses, the Pope immediately broke in and said: "In virtue of holy obedience, and under penalty of mortal sin, I command that you accept the dignity of the Cardinalate."

XXXIV.

N the Cardinalate he determined for himself that firstly, he could not change his mode of living in regard to the sparingness of his diet, his prayer, meditation, daily Mass and other statutes and customs of the Society; secondly, to not accumulate money nor enrich relatives, but to give whatever was superfluous from what was received to Churches or the poor; thirdly, not to ask more to be given him from the Pope, nor to accept the offices of Princes; all of these he kept.

XXXV.

IN the year 1602, when the Church of Capua was empty, the Pope gave it to N. He consecrated him on the second Sunday after Easter, when the Gospel *Ego sum Pastor bonus* is read, and after two days, gave to him the Archiepiscopal Pallium.

On the following day he left the palace and closed himself in the Roman College for four days, that he might flee visitors; and when he gave an exhortation to the brethren on Friday, soon after he left for residence in his Church.

This very hasty departure from the city brought admiration to many, and to the Pope himself, because a great many curial officials could hardly be plucked out from the curia, and another Cardinal who was consecrated with N. who was the Archbishop of Bari, delayed his departure even to the end of October.

XXXVI.

N. arrived in the Capuan Church on the first day of May, and, after carrying out a solemn entrance and having sung solemn Mass, a little later, that is, on the feast of the Ascension, he ascended the pulpit, and began his sermon.

In that first year he restored the Cathedral Church and the episcopal palace to a better form, costing thousands in gold; he wrote down a number of poor families, and in individual months he sent to them a certain amount of money; and he assigned monthly almsgiving in various pious places, apart from those which were given each day near the gate and from impromptu almsgiving.

For the three years that he resided in Capua, he visited the whole diocese three times; he celebrated three diocesan synods and once a provincial council, which had not been celebrated for eighteen years.

He found a custom that in the Cathedral a sermon was not given except for the four Sundays of Advent and through Lent; however, he began to preach on Christmas also, and nearly every Sunday of the year; not only in the city, but in country areas when making visitation. Since he could not be in both the country and in the city for the whole year, when he was in the city, he sent two fathers of the Society of Jesus that went around to the country folk, having ten gold pieces which were assigned to them for each month lest they should burden the country folk. When he would visit the country folk himself, these fathers remained in the city preaching and hearing confessions.

XXXVII.

N. wrote while he was in a certain rural area, an explanation of the creed in Italian, which he entrusted to the printers so that parish priests who did not know how to preach could read the explanation of one article after the Gospel, especially when it coincided with the feast days.

He also found a custom in use for both the canons and the parish priests to send expensive gifts to the Archbishop on Christmas, so he altogether forbade this custom, both so that the poor canons and the parish priests would not be weighed down, and so that the rich would give more to the poor and so have greater merit than they would if they were to give to the Archbishop who was not needy. He often thought and impressed upon others that verse of Isaiah: "Blessed is he who shakes his hand free of every bribe."[19]

He was present at the divine office with the canons (for the Archbishop of Capua is also a canon, and receives very plump stipends), on every feast day, not only for Mass and Vespers, but also for Matins and Lauds. Moreover, he was present on weekdays at least for Matins, not only to sustain the canons in the office and to become accustomed to serious and sober psalmody, but also to earn stipends for the poor, for he distributed them all to the poor; he said this alone is properly his own to make almsgiving with, which he earned naturally from his own labor, since the rest was the Church's, not his own.

---

[19] Isaiah 33:15.

XXXVIII.

HE foretold from the beginning that he was going to be in charge of that Church for only three years, and with great diligence investigated the names of his predecessors from St. Priscus, a disciple of St. Peter the Apostle, even to his own time, and placing all his predecessors in a catalogue of his most immediate predecessor, he said: "Cesare Costa sat for thirty years," and added: "N. sat for three years." And so it came to pass, as after the third year Pope Clement VIII died and his successor Paul V refused to allow N. to return to Capua and for that reason he was compelled to renounce his Church.

Hence, N. read the lives of the holy Bishops that he had gathered from Surius into one book; and he felt himself assisted by this reading. He was loved by the people and he himself loved the people; the royal ministers[20] also never inflicted any trouble upon him, rather, they venerated him, because they reckoned that he was a true servant of God.

---

[20] Capua was technically in the kingdom of Naples, which was under Spanish control and ruled by a viceroy in the city of Naples. –Translator's note.

XXXIX.

WHEN he was in the conclave that elected Leo XI, and again in the one that elected Paul V, he spent as much time as possible in his cell or alone in a solitary place praying the rosary or reading some little book, and privately in his prayers he said to the Lord: "*Mitte quem missurus es,*" and: "*A Papatu libera me Domine.*"[21] In the second conclave he was not far away from becoming Pope, and when some very serious man promised his service, N. exhorted him to desist, affirming that he did not need any favors, for if the act of picking up a bit of straw from the ground would make him Pope, it would stay where it lay. He had no hatred for those that tried to impede him nor was he disturbed by them; for he said the definition of the Papacy is perilous labor, or laborious danger.

In the time of Paul V, he expended scudi on the making of his title ... Likewise, the college of the Society at Montepulciano donated an income of fifty scudi in perpetuity; N. wanted to resign the Capuan Abbacy rendering more than a thousand scudi to the Capuan College, but the Pope would not allow it; still the proposer was able to give the Church the house and the garden of his Abbey.

At the same time he published his commentaries on the Psalms, two little books, or

---

[21] Respectively, "Send the one that you are going to send"; and "deliver me from the Papacy O Lord."
–Translator's note.

three in Italian, against the Doctors of Venice; likewise, an apologetic book against the king of England, a book against William Barclay, a book against Roger Widdrington, and a book on Ecclesiastical writers with a chronology.

XL.

N. was enrolled in many congregations of Cardinals, viz. the Holy Office, of the Index of Forbidden Books, the Congregation of Rites, on Examinations of Bishops, on indulgences, on the Propaganda Fidei, Germany, and Hungary. He was the Protector of the order of the Celestines, of St. Martha and the German College, and in turn protector *in absentia* for Cardinal Aldobrandini of the Charity of St. Jerome and of the *Convertitae*.

He still lives at seventy-one years old, and daily, chiefly in the month of September, gathers himself that he might be free for prayer and silence, after putting aside all occupations, that he might wipe away what he had contracted from so much business like dust, if he could somehow, and prepares himself to offer an account of his stewardship to God. Pray for him.

XLI.

N. wrote these things at the request of a friend and brother in the year 1613, in the month of June. He spoke nothing of his virtues, because he does not know whether he truly has any; he was silent on his vices, because they are not worthy that they be written and would that they be found blotted out from God's book on the day of judgment. Amen.

Additions

XLII.

. felt it would be beneficial to him to carry out much study from the necessity of teaching what he had not learned, and on account of the gift of facility, which he had from God, to take, grasp, and explain everything; for he was compelled to teach Greek and the precepts of Rhetoric, and scholastic Theology, and in early youth to preach in Churches, and give exhortations to the brethren of his order.

Since he was compelled by such necessity, he learned Greek and Hebrew by himself, and read nearly all the Fathers, histories, and many scholastic Doctors, as well as Councils, and the chief labor of these, was nearly the whole body of Canon Law, for which he did not labor much to understand what he read, since particularly, in the different colleges he lived in, he always had someone to consult.

XLIII.

HE was sent to Naples to become acquainted with the writings of Fr. Salmeron. He remained in the city for nearly five months, namely from May to October; in that time he read the immense volumes of the aforesaid Father, and daily advanced to him errata that he had found either in authors he had cited or in false histories, or in new opinions, or things not rightly explained in the Scriptures, whether in dogmatic, philosophical or theological doctrines abhorring the truth.

Although, when the said Father first heard these things he became angry and tried to defend them, at length, on the following day he emended everything with a peaceful mind, and, unless I am mistaken, this acquaintance benefited him a great deal.

XLIV.

N the Belgian controversy of Fr. Lessius with the Louvain doctors, N. made no small labor to conciliate Cardinal Madrutius with the doctors of the Society. He wrote a short work for that, in which he showed the doctrine of the Society agrees with the doctrine of the old Louvain doctors, Tapperus, Tiletanus, and others, and that the more recent Louvain doctors do not rightly explain our doctrine.

XLV.

N regard to the book of Molina *de Concordia*, firstly N. admonished Father General, before the whole controversy *de auxiliis* [on efficacious grace] arose, that there were many propositions in Molina *male sonans*,[22] and he showed the writings to him. Fr. General sent these into Spain and thence a new edition of Fr. Molina followed, wherein he tried to soften them and said he spoke in a disputative manner, not in an assertive one. Then, after the quarrel on this question arose [with the Dominicans], N. was commanded by Pope Clement VIII to write what he thought on the censure of the Dominican Fathers, and he wrote a clear work in which he showed in what the whole controversy consisted, and that the opinion of the Dominicans was as dangerous as that of Molina.

That work was approved to a remarkable extent by the Pope in the beginning. He also wrote two other works answering the objections, or charges of our adversaries, which did not displease the Pope; and when N. was already a Cardinal at Tusculum, with the Pope himself, he gave a discourse on these matters, and the Pope called the opinion of the Society "our opinion",

---

[22] *Male sonans* is a Theological note, or censure, that is applied to a work by theologians and taken up by the Church herself to characterize a work that is not heretical but the language "sounds bad", as in it could cause confusion or scandal and thus should be revised. –Translator's note.

i.e., his and the Society's. But later he was completely changed, and so long as N. was at Rome, he refused publicly to treat on it lest N. himself might be present.

After N.'s departure,[23] he immediately wanted to discuss it in the presence of the Cardinals of the Holy Office. Still, N. himself often admonished the Pope to beware of frauds, and not to think that by his own study, since he was not a Theologian, he could arrive at the understanding of such an obscure matter; clearly he foretold to the him [Pope] that the question would not be defined by His Holiness, and when he repeated that he was going to define it, N. responded: "Your Holiness will not define it." He foretold the same thing to Cardinal del Monte,[24] who later recalled it to N.'s memory.

XLVI.

N. disagreed with Cardinal Baronius on a certain congregation on the reform of the Breviary, in regard to the passion of St. Andrew, whether it was truly written by a priest of Achaia; Baronius rejected this, but when he heard N.'s opinion and his

---

[23] Namely, St. Robert's appointment as Bishop to Capua. This has given some cause to suppose that the Pope wanted to remove Bellarmine from the discussion on this question. –Translator's note.

[24] Cardinal Maria del Monte is also known for being the first patron of the famous artist Caravaggio. –Translator's note.

reasons, he said publicly that he lost the case, and N.'s opinion pleased him more than his own.

XLVII.

E did many things for the beatification of St. Ignatius. The first was that he brought the memorial of the general congregation, at which he was present, to Cardinal Gesualdus, the prefect of the Congregation of Sacred Rites, and so introduced the cause of canonization.

Then, he gave the first exhortation on the praises of St. Ignatius in the Church of the professed house, in the presence of Fathers and brothers, with Cardinal Baronius present; at the end of the exhortation, Cardinal Baronius sought an image of St. Ignatius and, after going up a ladder, affixed it above the tomb of the same Blessed Father, then he began to honor and frequent the tomb. Later, when the time seemed opportune to him to seek the beatification, he advised Fr. General, and Fr. General saw to it with great care that Fr. Procurator would quickly obtain those things which were necessary and advance the business in the shortest possible time. If this had not been done, especially at the urging of all the Cardinals of the congregation, and wholeheartedly proclaimed their vote, God knows when the beatification would have been obtained.[25]

---

[25] The Beatification of St. Ignatius took place in 1623, two years after St. Robert's death. –Translator's note.

XLVIII.

FOR Blessed Aloysius [Gonzaga], N. related to Pope Paul V, with Cardinals Ascoli and Pamphilji, that he was worthy to be distinguished with the name of Blessed. When Aloysius' body was near the tomb, he made an intervention to seek the faculty from Fr. General to place the body in a wooden coffin apart from the other bodies so that it could be recognized if he would be canonized at some point.[26]

Later, he subjected himself to examination for his canonization, and with other Cardinals of the Congregation of Rites, he procured remissorial letters. After he treated on the beatification, he himself first spoke abundantly on his innocence and austerity of life, as well as his miracles. He concluded that all the saints are so considered either due to innocence or penance, but St. Aloysius can be beatified on account of both, to the similitude of St. John the Baptist; and all the Cardinals followed his will, and the decree came to pass, which still the Supreme Pontiff has not confirmed, and whatever the reason may be, it is not known.

FINIS

---

[26] The practice of the early Jesuits was that all bodies would be wrapped in linen and laid in common graves. Thus, this particular intervention was out of the ordinary. –Translator's note.

ST. PETER'S BASILICA, CIRCA 1600

St. Peter's Basilica, as it was in St. Robert Bellarmine's time. The portico of the original Constantinian Basilica was still present on the outside, even though the original Church had fallen down and was replaced by the building we know today. At the end of St. Robert's life, the Dome, designed by Michaelangelo Buonarotti, and the facade would have been complete, but the obelisk and colonnade we see today were not yet in place.

A page from St. Robert Bellarmine's famous *Controversies*, from his work *de Monachis*, or *On Monks*, corrected at the bottom in his own hand.

POPE SIXTUS V

Pope Clement VIII

Above Cathedral Church in Capua, renovated by St. Robert Bellarmine

Left. The mitre St. Robert wore as Archbishop of Capua.

St. Robert Bellarmine teaching catechism in his titular Church of *Santa Maria in Via*.

St. Robert Bellarmine and St. Aloyisius Gonzaga

Appendix A
The Roman College and Scholastic Disputation

HE Roman College, which we today call the Gregorium, was originally founded by St. Ignatius in 1541. It was his heart's desire, and he planned and nourished his project through all the naysayers and great opposition. He even managed to obtain from Pope Paul IV, who never had any liking for the saint, the right to confer their own degrees; or in other words, their degrees were legal doctorates. The Roman College was also free to all who entered, which means it very quickly became filled beyond capacity in both classes and housing.

To even get to this stage, however, a student needed to have passed through what were called Grammar Schools. These trained young boys in grammar (which meant learning Latin rather than their own language's higher grammar), logic, and rhetoric. In this period, *eloquentia Latina* was the only thing that mattered; if one knew Latin he was educated, and if he did not, then he was not considered educated. So Grammar was the means whereby one learned how to speak and read Latin, Logic trained someone to argue correctly in Latin, and Rhetoric taught one how to sound good while doing it. The next effect was a wide exposure to reading and various periods of history—at this time the Greco-Roman period above all—as well as famous writers, principally Cicero. Latin was taught by natural methods rather than what can be called the "death by grammar" approach adopted in the 19th century so as to make Latin grammar a "science" in that enlightenment sense. Unfortunately such books still plague most Latin curriculums today.

Then, when beginning studies at any University, such as the Roman College, one would be prepared by that Latin fluency to not only understand the lectures, but to read the material at hand and commentaries on it, all of which was written in Latin. Still, we must add that the Roman College also contained Grammar schools for the poorest boys in the city. In many ways it was a grammar school, public school, college and seminary all rolled into one.

Moreover, the student body of most Universities was not made up exclusively of the native population, but often had numerous students from other countries. St. Thomas Aquinas and St. Bonaventure were both Italians studying, and later teaching, at the University of Paris, yet they never spoke any French because Latin was sufficient to speak with their fellow religious as well as their students. This was unchanged in the 1560s when St. Robert Bellarmine entered the Roman college, which likewise had an international attendance, and it was not limited only to Jesuits. English and German students featured very prominently, especially in the time that Bellarmine taught Controversial Theology there. Catholics were forbidden to attend the Universities of England

and suffered great persecution in the Protestant areas of Germany.

As we will have seen from the first few pages of the *Autobiography*, St. Robert was supremely proficient in Latin from his grammar school days. He also delighted in the study of astronomy and medicine. In this way he was perfectly prepared for studies at the Roman College, which could be described as Aristotle—for Aristotle dominated every subject. The 16th Century University offered two doctorates, just as its medieval forerunners, one in Philosophy and one in Theology. The only exception to this were Canonists, who received the *Juris Doctor* that is still used today. Interestingly, this system survives in modern doctorates, where one gets a *Philosophae Doctor* or PhD, even if it is for matters as diverse as history and biology, while for Theology one receives a *Sacrae Theologiae Doctor*, or STD.

To obtain the doctorate in Philosophy, a rigorous course in Aristotle was the order of the day. Though denigrated by proponents of modern educational theory, Aristotle was not the tyrant of those who want to know, even if the Latin translations were not as good as they could have been. They reproduced the course of Logic in the grammar schools but on a higher level, based on Aristotle's *Organon*, then running to numerous other subjects of human knowledge through Aristotle's books on Astronomy and the Physics, and ethics, then to the queen of all Philosophy, where Aristotle is arguably at his best, Metaphysics. St. Robert, in spite of frequent illnesses, would always stand out amongst his schoolmates.

Another feature of the events he speaks of are the public disputations. These were not much different from how medical dissections would be viewed for entertainment in places such as Bologna and Amsterdam. Men had been addicted to public disputations for centuries and they were wildly popular. Such disputations would have a group of masters or doctors that were to defend various positions against those who would scrutinize their knowledge, and prospective masters almost always had a *praesides* (president) that led and argued for them. St. Robert never loved philosophy for its own sake and rather more preferred Theology because this is where the war for souls was to be waged. Nevertheless, he was always able to defend philosophical points, and it is clear reading the impact and importance Aristotle's Logic had in his Theological works.

After his own order, the Roman College was perhaps the place most loved by St. Robert. In 1594 he became the Rector of the College, and would often lavish alms upon it to help poor students eat.

Appendix B
The French Wars of Religion and Henri Bourbon

We now come to the most complicated of the historical events of Bellarmine's time, the French Wars of Religion. Of these there were seven, and it was during the sixth that Bellarmine was sent to France.

The wars began with John Calvin's offensive in the Affair of the Placards. Calvin, being a lawyer from Normandy, and an academic, decided he would show the rabble of Paris how foolish the "Popish" doctrines were, so he put up many signs (placards) over Paris blaspheming the Blessed Sacrament, the veneration of the saints, processions, relics, and the Mass. Calvin gravely miscalculated. Whatever the Parisian Catholics knew about the Catechism is quite in doubt; many were illiterate, and even those who were not did not concern themselves much with doctrine or theology, in spite of the world famous university in their midst. What mattered for the lay Catholic in Paris was not points of doctrine or Catechism, or even questions of justification, but rather the Mass, the Blessed Sacrament, processions, saints' days and relics. To see these things blasphemed was an affront that left a permanent distaste for Calvinism in the mouth of the average Parisian, even until the French Revolution. King François I was forced to take punitive measures against the Calvinists, and thus began the great conflict of Calvinists

(Huguenots) throughout France. François' line, however, was very weak, and many of his descendants were sickly and died young. By the 1580s the line had been reduced to Henri III, who was perceived by the people to be weak against Calvinism.

In the meantime, we must mention Henri Bourbon. Tangentially connected to the royal line by his father, Henri was born in Navarre and became that country's king. His mother, Jeanne d'Albret, uprooted Catholicism from the people more cruelly than a Henry VIII or an Elizabeth, and inculcated Calvinism in her young son. Henri became a great athlete and a bold man, and in 1569 became the head of the Calvinist party in France. The possibility of his succession to the French throne had not come to anyone's mind just yet, and the St. Bartholomew's Massacre had cowed him into converting to Catholicism. The St. Bartholomew's massacre is often used to attack the Church, but that is in the absence of attention given to other massacres committed by the Calvinists in other areas of France. The other problem is that what defines a "massacre" is often a politically motivated affair, as we see in US history where 5 people were shot dead by British soldiers whom they taunted and threatened, and it is called a "massacre". The same issue was then present in France when one or the other side claimed a massacre had taken place, albeit that of St. Bartholomew was indeed a massacre. Far from being an event orchestrated by the Church, it was orchestrated by the crown under Henri II to eliminate Calvinist influence in government by killing the Admiral Coligny. When people found out what was going on they spontaneously took it as an occasion to take revenge and settle old scores, not to mention the memory of Calvinist attacks on Catholic cities were fresh in their minds. Thus ignited the fifth Religious War which was ended by the Peace of Monsieur in 1576.

Still, the Calvinists received various concessions and the Catholics of the country feared new massacres. So they established the Catholic League, which was a loose connection of armies and militias from various neighboring towns and cities lead by Henri, the Duke of Guise. The new king, Henri III, did not much care for the League, like a Saul faced with the glory of a David, yet he had no alternative. Then enter the third Henri, namely Henri Bourbon, now relapsed to Calvinism and head of the Calvinist leagues forming to defend against the Catholic majority.

Apart from the affair of the three Henris, there was one more factor, namely, that the king's brother, the Duke Anjou, had died, leaving Henri III childless and far south of anything morally upright as the last of the Valois line; Henri Bourbon was then heir to the throne.

Now the situation came to Pope Sixtus V's attention. The imperious Sixtus V, for all his fiery temper, was first and foremost dedicated to the independence of the Church from secular influence or anything that smacked of Caesaropapism. It was Sixtus' singular achievement to liberate the papacy from the domination of the Spanish, which Pius V and Gregory XIII had allowed in exchange for defense against the Turks.

Sixtus had watched the situation from afar, and somewhat admired Henri Bourbon, for he is said to have had admiration for strong resolute men such as himself. Nevertheless, the ambassadors of the Spanish King, Philip II, very heavily argued that Sixtus should excommunicate Bourbon, lest a heretic would wear the crown of St. Louis. The Spanish angle in this was not altogether disinterested. Philip II's third wife was Elizabeth Valois, and his daughter, the Infanta, was half French and thus naturally an heir to the throne of France, as far as Philip was concerned. The truth is, however, that on account of Salic law, the Infanta could not succeed by the claims of her mother, but this did not stop Philip. His real aim was to dominate his great rival, and short of that, to see to her dismemberment, with a large portion of it bestowed on him and the rest upon his cousins in the Holy Roman Empire.

It was not only the Spanish but many others that felt that Henri Bourbon, the King of Navarre, would never convert and thus could never be allowed to wear the crown of France. So at last, in September 1585, the Pope published a Bull declaring Henri Bourbon a heretic and thus incapable of succeeding the throne of France.

Meanwhile the League grew from a modest confederation, mostly among the aristocracy, to a well disciplined and organized force with numerous volunteers now well trained and devoted to the Catholic faith. On the other hand, in Paris a party appeared called the *Politiques*, who were of largely Gallican sentiment and supported the claims of Henri Bourbon. Then, Bourbon and the league were at open war throughout the country. The penultimate religious war was on, and France was in great danger of going the way of England.

To make matters worse, Henri III, less than pleased with the Catholic League, came into open conflict with the Guises, who were at its head, and determined to assassinate the duke and his brother, who was a Cardinal, while taking another Cardinal, Charles Bourbon (a distant relation of Henri Bourbon, and well behind him in the line of succession), and putting him in prison. This was a grave miscalculation, however, because word quickly got out and the people turned against the king. Henri's next move was to quit Paris and throw himself into the arms of the Huguenots. The royal forces now joined forces with Bourbon to bring rebellious Paris to heel. While outside the city with his troops in 1589, Henri III was assassinated by the dagger of a crazed Franciscan named Jacques Clément. The country was kingless, and the contest was now between Henri Bourbon and Charles Bourbon, the former a Calvinist whose royal blood was his chief support, and the potential Charles X, whose only real claim was the support of the Catholic League.

In the midst of all this trouble, which saw France more divided than even in the times of St. Joan of Arc, Pope Sixtus V acted. He sent a legation to France for the purpose of uniting all the Catholic elements of the country. Sixtus appointed Cardinal Cajetan for this task, and since many issues of Theology and Canon Law might arise, he sent along St. Robert Bellarmine as his principal advisor, along with several others. Thus Bellarmine enters this complicated story, and the narrative of the autobiography ensues. [Paragraph XXVII].

During the time in which Bellarmine was in Paris the city was besieged by Henri Bourbon. Paris was ill-prepared and soon dogs and cats became rather scarce, boiled shoe-leather being the order of the day. We know from the early biographers that St. Robert gave exhortations to the people daily to keep up their strength, and gave his small offerings of food to the poor while putting his hunger out of mind by laboring in the great libraries of the city. Moreover, the priests heard confessions every day in preparation for what seemed inevitable. Yet Paris held out until the Catholic League and the Spanish could come to the rescue, and Bourbon found it necessary to abandon the siege. It is at this point that what Bellarmine relates about receiving the letter informing Cardinal Cajetan of Pope Sixtus' death occurs as well as the subsequent departure.

The Catholic League tried very hard to call an Estates General to set aside Salic law in favor of marriage accession by the Spanish Infanta, but Henri Bourbon pulled the rug out from under the League by his conversion back to Catholicism. It is related that Bourbon declared, "*Paris vaut une Masse.*" (Paris is worth a Mass), and as a result, moderates and many members of the League dropped all their opposition to Bourbon and he was thus made King Henri IV, whom the French would remember as their most beloved king in spite of the sordid history leading up to his coronation—largely due to the sordid history of his successors. Pope Clement VIII was convinced by Cardinal Baronius, St. Robert's great friend, to accept Henri's conversion, contrary to Spanish protests, and confirm him as king, which was duly done, and France began the slow recovery as a nation.

Appendix C
St. Robert Bellarmine, Sixtus V and the Vulgate

As mentioned in the last appendix, Sixtus V was strong and resolute and had preserved the independence of the Church. Yet, at the same time, he imposed his resolute will within the Church in any place he turned his attention. The first place was the Jesuits. Sixtus was the first Pope for whom the Jesuits had existed throughout his adult life and thus they had taken their place among the historic orders. Consequently, Sixtus felt it was his place to reform the Jesuits, particularly on the issue of their absolute obedience. The Jesuit Superior, Claudio Aquaviva, was politely, yet resolutely, resisting Sixtus' efforts, which irritated him greatly. It was in this mood that his attention was turned to St. Robert, who was away on his legation to France.

St. Robert had assisted Pope Sixtus in the past on the latter's critical edition of the letters of St. Ambrose. It happens to be one of the worst editions because Sixtus ignored all critical advice and became very irritated when anyone would correct him. Sixtus was also a Canonist, and among the body of Canon Lawyers of that time it was popular to interpret the teachings and actions of Popes such as Innocent III, Gregory VII and Boniface VIII with the view that the Pope was in fact the Lord of the world directly and all kings his vassals. St. Robert had attacked this view, though with no intent to do anything other than write the truth, in his work *On the Roman Pontiff,* book 5, which is the shortest of that whole work, yet caused the most trouble throughout his life in one way or another. Bellarmine held that the Pope possessed temporal power, outside of his domain in the Papal States, indirectly. This meant that the Pope could depose or otherwise inflict penalties on kings for the sake of the faith, but not arbitrarily, and likewise outside of questions of faith and morals, secular laws would take precedence over Ecclesiastical ones. He also added a number of authorities from the Church Fathers and the Scholastics, including Hugh of St. Victor, St. Thomas Aquinas, and St. Bonaventure.

Various canonists came to Sixtus and expressed their displeasure. Now, Sixtus, who fought aggressively for the rights of the Church against the temporal powers, came to view St. Robert's opinion as dangerous to the authority of the Papacy. Thus he moved to put the whole of the Controversies on the Index of Forbidden books. Many people intervened to stop this, including the Spanish government, as Sixtus wanted to put the Spanish Dominican, Victoria, on the Index for the same proposition. The Congregation of the Index found nothing contrary to the faith in Bellarmine's work, but Sixtus would not be moved.[27] As a result he put

---

[27] It is related, albeit perhaps sarcastically, by the Spanish Ambassador that the Congregation of the Index feared to tell the Pope that Bellarmine and Victoria's positions were supported by numerous

St. Robert's work on the Index of Forbidden Books, along with that of Victoria. This volume may still be seen in the Vatican Apostolic Library, numbered only on odd pages. This was, however, never formally promulgated. Just before the promulgation of this edition of the Index, in 1590, Sixtus died, and the next Pope, Urban VII, immediately had Bellarmine and Victoria removed from the very odd company with which they might be placed.

As an epilogue to this interesting story, it is worth noting that while Bellarmine's teaching on the indirect power of the Pope was not enough for Sixuts, it was too much in other quarters. Bellarmine's public debate via books with King James I of England over the oath of allegiance also revolved around this teaching, and in France the Gallican party long had a hatred of St. Robert on account of his view of papal authority.

Another issue addressed in the Autobiography is the question of the Sixtine Vulgate. Bellarmine relates that under Pope Clement VIII, work began in earnest to correct errors that had crept in. Firstly we must address the nature of this reform, then we can turn to address how this passage of the Autobiography was used against him by some detractors.

1) The Council of Trent had decreed that the Vulgate, due to its long use throughout the life of the Church, was infallible in Faith and Morals.

---

saints lest the Pope would put the saints themselves on the index. Couderc, *Le Vénérable Cardinal Bellarmin*, t. 1, p. 132; cited in Broderick, *The Life and Writings of Blessed Robert Bellarmine*, pp. 270-71.

Yet the Council Fathers were well aware of the textual issues and copyist errors that had crept into the Vulgate. Printing was still relatively new in this time, and the Bible had been copied by hand for centuries; consequently, errors had crept in via copiers.

2) As a result, the Council had also decreed that the Vulgate needed to be reformed.

This commission was duly prepared under Pope Gregory XIII, and Bellarmine was on the commission. They labored very hard and produced many wonderful results, but then Pope Sixtus V was elected, and he decided to take on the project personally. He began with what Bellarmine describes in the Autobiography as the Louvain Bible, namely, the Bible of the Dutch scholar Hentenius, which at that time was held to be one of the more accurate manuscripts. Then, Sixtus decided to depart from the system of versification, which had been standard for some time. Sixtus had, of course, devised a more logical system of versification, yet it was rather imprudent for two reasons. One of them was that men had become used to them and referring to them, and countless books would have to be edited to adjust to the new system. The bigger problem is that it would leave the Church open to the Protestant attack—here indeed would be proof that the Church changed the Bible. Of course it would not have, but it would make for excellent propaganda. Then, Sixtus refused to take advice from anyone and went to revise the text entirely on his own. Though he was a good scholar in his own right, it was simply too big of a job for any man. The result was that Sixtus left out whole verses in some places, though purely by accident, as they had no impact on any matter of faith or morals. Sixtus V had the Bull of Promulgation prepared, and was constantly making more and more revisions which pushed the date of promulgation back again and again. The whole Catholic world waited in anticipation through the hot summer months of 1590—and then the bells tolled for Sixtus' death.

The next three Popes, Urban VII, Gregory XIV and Innocent IX all died within the next year (1591), and at last Pope Clement VIII was elected, who would reign for 12 years. Gregory XIV was the first to deal with this problem in his very short reign, and called in the theologians from Cardinal Zagarolo's original commission to suggest a plan. Bellarmine suggested a plan of action not to forbid or condemn Sixtus' Vulgate, but to work very quickly to correct it, and replace it with the revised version. Gregory XIV approved the plan but died before anything substantial could be done, and the next Popes did not live long either. Thus it fell to Pope Clement to bring the project to completion.

Clement had St. Philip Neri as a spiritual director, and immediately saw the danger to the Church of not repairing the problems inherent in Sixtus' edition of the Vulgate, so he assisted the work as much as possible. The Theologians worked very quickly but diligently, going back to the Hentenius edition, as he says in the Autobiography, and restoring the older versification and dealing with some questions of textual criticism. When the work was promulgated, it was under the name of Pope Sixtus, and later had Clement's name added to it, and was the Bible in use in the Universal Church until the revision of the New Vulgate begun under Pius XII, which took a very different course following the 1960s. It certainly deserves its own book, but we could not possibly address it here. The edition of Clement VIII however is still used in the 1962 Missal and Breviary.

2) Now we return to St. Robert. In his plan for salvaging the situation, he relates that he had said: "What should be done, then, was that the inadvisable changes should be abolished as quickly as possible, and the Bible reprinted under the name of the same Sixtus, with a preface added to it wherein it will be shown that in the first edition of Sixtus, due to haste, some errors crept in whether of the printers or of other persons." (Pg. 35) On account of this, some detractors objected in the 1923 process for his beatification that St. Robert lied, and as a result could not be a saint. While it is certainly true that smacks of a mental reservation, it was by no means a lie. Sixtus V most certainly worked in great haste, and he was most certainly constantly changing and making revisions. It is probably also true that errors crept in through the printers. In all events, it is as St. Ambrose had said about Jacob, in that part of Genesis where he presents himself to his father Isaac as though he were Esau, "It is a mystery rather than a lie."

For more information on this interesting and complicated chapter of history, there is a lengthy analysis in Broderick, *The Life and Writings of Blessed Robert Bellarmine*, vol. 1, pp 277-309, and the phenomenal work by Fr. Xavier Marie Bachelet, *Bellarmin et la Bible Sixto-Clémentine: étude et documents inédits,* upon which this Appendix is based.

A Guide to Composing Sermons

I. The purpose of a Christian preacher ought to be to faithfully teach the people that which they ought, or would be fitting for them, to know about divine doctrine. At the same time, he ought to move them to attain virtues and flee vices.

II. This is why it is necessary that anyone that is going to preach should, first of all, set before him the scope to which he means to direct his whole action and its individual parts; *e.g.* he ought to say to himself: Today's Gospel exhorts to penance. Therefore, I mean to labor, with God's help, that I might implant the desire for true penance, and for that reason I shall gather the reasons, advantages, examples and other such things which will help to obtain this end. For equal reason, he should examine the individual parts of his sermon, and see whether they will bring about the proposed end.

Moreover, many not only preach uselessly, but even with danger to their souls, who propose no scope for themselves but to wrap up in about an hour, some with melodious opinions, some by a variety of matters and words to the delight of their hearers. For these, as they do not have a true purpose that has been proposed, also do not obtain anything, although they labor and tire themselves out a great deal.

III. To teach one of the ends of the preacher: it is not enough for him to say something on individual phrases of the Gospel, or conceived from individual words, as they call it, to elicit certain things as some do who do not preach the word of God but their own words; rather, it is necessary to draw out the true, germane, and literal sense and thence to confirm dogmas of faith or hand down precepts of life, and briefly to teach that which the Holy Spirit meant to be taught by those words.

For that is what it means to shepherd and instruct the people in the word of God. The Fathers that must be read for their exposition of Scripture could be sought from my Catalogue.[1] From more recent preachers, it seems to me that Cornelius Jansen and Adam Sasbout excel.

IV. To move to the zeal for virtues, which is the other purpose of the preacher, it is not enough for him to get angry and cry out against sinners, for empty shouts may sometimes terrify the more simple, but the wiser will hold them in ridicule, and certainly they will produce fruit in neither.

Therefore, it is necessary to first convince the mind of his hearers with solid reasons which are adduced from the divine testimonies, from causes and effects of the things which he is treating, and chiefly by placing examples and like things, that they be compelled to affirm that it must seem to them as the preacher says; and then by copious

---

[1] *De Scriptoribus Ecclesiasticis.*

and efficacious words, as well as by various examples, the listeners are impelled that they would wish in earnest to know what they ought to will.

To discover reasons and examples of this sort, the digressions of St. John Chrysostom in the Epistles of St. Paul can help a great deal, as well as the sermons of the same writer *To the People of Antioch*; the sermons of St. Basil *on Fasting et seq.*, the sermons of St. Augustine on the Psalms, the sermons on the Lord's words and on the words of the Apostle [Paul], as well as other homilies of this sort; the *Dialogue* of St. Gregory, and all the ecclesiastical histories, and chiefly, the books on the lives of the saints written by St. Athanasius, Suplicius, Jerome, Palladius, Theodoret, Bede and others.

V. There are three things necessary for anyone who wishes to preach usefully: zeal for God, or the spirit and fervor for charity; wisdom and eloquence, which are signified by the fiery tongues which appeared over the Apostles when they were made the first preachers of the Gospel by God; ardor designates the zeal of fire; splendor, wisdom; the form of the tongue, eloquence. Eloquence without charity and wisdom is the sounding gong and empty chattering. Wisdom and eloquence without charity is a mundane human affair, and dead. Charity without wisdom and eloquence is the nature of a strong but toothless man.

VI. To draw zeal for the spirit, for which a Christian preacher ought chiefly to be zealous, nothing is more beneficial than regular prayer and constant and serious thought of heavenly things.

VII. Three things are required of the preacher for necessary wisdom. The first is the knowledge of the Scriptures, and therefore, preachers ought to read something from the divine Scripture daily, that they might become very familiar with it, and at the same time consult the commentaries of the Fathers. Secondly, knowledge of ecclesiastical dogmas is required, of which the safest kind is the doctrine of St. Thomas and the Catechism of the Council of Trent. For all that, those who propose the opinions of the Doctors on doctrines do not act rightly; it would be more than sufficient if the people could grasp and plainly understand those which are certain. Thirdly, diverse erudition is required, that he might have plenty of examples and reasons, which are sought from histories and the books of the Fathers.

VIII. For Christian eloquence, nay more, for all true eloquence, it is required that skill should improve and polish, but not destroy or corrupt nature. Usually sins are especially committed in this one matter. Skill ought to improve nature because sometimes several speak and act viciously either from education or from another source, as when they use improper words or those less genuine, or obscure phrases, and when they move their head in an undignified manner or make gestures with their left hand, or otherwise sin in act. Such vices can and ought to be easily known and avoided. Again, skill ought, as I said, not destroy nature; and if some lapses must be tolerated, it is less evil to not correct them than to destroy nature. Those who destroy nature when they preach, either use an insolent tone of voice, so that they do not seem to speak but recite, or sing; or they use poetic or excessively emotional words; or certainly such phrases in their sermons that everyone might reckon that they labored very much in composing the sermon. For these sorts of things take away nearly all the authority of the preacher.

IX. If anyone would put vice to flight, he ought to consider that, although he is going to speak to many from a higher place, nevertheless, he is going to speak with each man individually, and that he will so act with them as if he were addressing them apart. For when someone speaks with one man, to persuade him of something, certainly he does not use many epithets in the beginning, nor poetic phrases, nor a strange voice, nor movement of the limbs; but by plain human custom, first while the body is at rest with a moderated voice and with simple opinions; then, if it is necessary to contend or rebuke, he raises his voice, multiplies words, agitates the body, cries out, etc., that from the change of voice and the commotion of the members he might get results, not by affectation or artifice. This alone ought to be the difference between the sermon of the preacher to the people and a familiar discussion of one to another, that the preacher, to be heard suitably, is to speak more loftily and even more seriously, and more considerately, on account of the honor of the multitude, for the multitude is honorable.

X. There are three kinds of sermons found in use among the Fathers of the Church; some explain the Scriptures in order in their sermon and diligently explain individual opinions. Such are the treatises of St. Augustine on Job, Basil on the Hexameron, Chrysostom on Genesis; these propose only to teach: for they mix in affects only briefly and in passing. Others are wholly given to treating common passages, such as the sermons of Chrysostom to the people of Antioch, the sermons of Basil of diverse arguments, and a great many sermons of Augustine, Leo, and other Fathers, and these chiefly look to the motion of the passions. Others partly explain the Scriptures, and partly direct to commend virtues and detest vices; Chrysostom characteristically furnishes this in his homilies on the Epistles of Paul, and however much more briefly in Matthew, Job, and the Acts of the Apostles. St. Augustine did the same thing in the Psalms, after the thirtieth. These three types are useful and must be duly visited. The fourth several convey who treat on scholastic questions in the sermon; and the fifth, others, who tell the evangelical histories with exquisite words and flowery rhetoric, or amplify the crimes of the Pharisees or dispute on more subtle matters, or speak on other matters of this sort with inept skill and great labor without any utility.

Characteristic books are extant on ecclesiastical rhetoric or on making sermons, of Cardinal Augustine of Verona, Didacus Stella, Aloysius of Granada, Alphonsus Zorilla and of others, from whom the precepts can be sought in particular on individual parts of the sermon.

SERMONS OF ST. ROBERT BELLARMINE

Super Missus Est Angelus
On the Annunciation

Translated from:
Opera Oratoria Posthuma

First Sermon Super Missus Est

Given on the First Sunday of Advent
3 December 1610

What must be considered: a) the time of legation; b) the person sending; c) the person to whom he is sent; d) the person which is sent; e) the business.

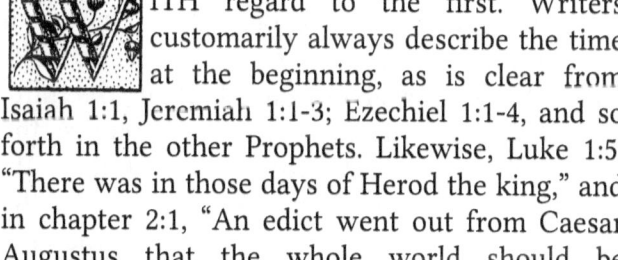ITH regard to the first. Writers customarily always describe the time at the beginning, as is clear from Isaiah 1:1, Jeremiah 1:1-3; Ezechiel 1:1-4, and so forth in the other Prophets. Likewise, Luke 1:5, "There was in those days of Herod the king," and in chapter 2:1, "An edict went out from Caesar Augustus that the whole world should be enrolled," and 3:1, "In the fifteenth year of the

Emperor Tiberius Caesar." So now, he begins in 1:26, "He was sent in the sixth month." Note by these words firstly, the time that has elapsed from the conception of John the Baptist. Wherein there is a mystery: John is conceived when all things wither, the leaves fall, the fruit is finished, etc.; Christ is conceived when all things are born, in vigor and in flower, etc.

John signifies the law, which will be finished, as well as all the ceremonies, sacrifices, and figures that were withering; Christ signifies the Gospel which is in vigor, etc. Likewise, John is born when the days begin to get shorter; but Christ when they begin to get longer. John signifies the old man, Christ the new, etc. For that reason, by a great mystery, Christ and John divide between themselves four principal days of the whole year.

But additionally, just as this legation happens in the sixth month, so it also happens in the sixth age of the world, which is also the last. For just as the world was made in six days, and then came the rest on the Sabbath, so the world will endure the onset of six ages, then there will be eternal rest. The first age was the infancy, as it were, from Adam even to Noah; the second, like childhood from Noah even to Abraham; the third, like adolescence, from Abraham to Moses; the fourth, like youth from Moses to David; the fifth, like manhood from David even to Christ; the sixth, like old age from Christ even to the end. For that reason, Paul calls it the fullness of time, "When the fullness of time came, God sent His

Son,"² since without a doubt the last age came. St. John calls this the last hour: "It is the last hour."³ And in the Epistle for the first Sunday of Advent: "Now is the hour to rise from sleep; night has passed and day has approached,"⁴ because the last hour, of which John speaks, is not the last of the day, but of the night, because the whole time of this world is the night in respect to the coming age.

Why did Christ wait so long? 1) Because God willed the magnitude of human weakness to be understood, which could not be cured either by natural reason, or philosophers, nor even by patriarchs and prophets, etc.; 2) Because he wished the magnitude of this mystery to be understood. Therefore, he wished it first to be prefigured and promised to many and by various ways. An example would be the arrival of a great King, whom many precursors, messengers, and beasts of burden laden with furniture precede. Think how great he is, whom servants and laden animals precede for five thousand years.

From there we proceed to the second consideration. The person sending is God: "The Angel Gabriel was sent by God." Why is it God? Who will explain it? We can hunt for solutions from three sources: 1) from names; 2) from creatures; 3) from the Scriptures. The name of God in Italian and Latin comes from Greek. In Greek the learned assign it as Θεός [Theos], and it

---

² Galatians 4:4.
³ 1 John 2:18.
⁴ Romans 13:11.

means three things according to Theodoret⁵ and St. John Damascene.⁶ Θεός is said to be from θεωρεῖν [theōrein] *i.e.* "to see", θέειν [theein] *i.e.* "to run", αἴθειν [aithein], *i.e.* "to burn", and they are in conformity with the Hebrew names. One of the names of God, as Jerome witnesses,⁷ is Elijion, *i.e.* "the most high". For, he who is in a higher place sees many more things than one in a lower place. For that reason, Paul says: "All things are naked and uncovered before his eyes."⁸ Therefore, God has this as his own, that he sees all things, and that description does not fit any creature. For men do not see many things which his eyes see. The angels do not see many things, such as those things that are free, and human thoughts and wills. Moreover, God sees all things, "You alone know all the hearts of the sons of men."⁹ For, the eye of God is of infinite subtlety. Therefore, he penetrates the inscrutable heart of man; nay more, he even sees what is going to be free, which we ourselves do not see, as is clear from the denial of Peter. "You have foreseen all my paths, and understood my thoughts from afar. Your knowledge of me is wonderful, it has grown lofty and I am not able to come to it."¹⁰

---

[5] Theodoret, *serm. 3 ad Graecos*; *De cur. Graec.* aff. III: MG 83, 864.
[6] *De Fide Orthodoxa*, I, 9; MG 94, 837.
[7] *Epistola ad Marcellam de nominibus Dei*; Epist. 25; ML 22, 429.
[8] Hebrews 4:13.
[9] 2 Par. 6:30.
[10] Psalm 138:4-6.

Not only does God see all things, but he runs as fast as he sees is necessary. He surpasses all things with his speed, even the winds and lightning. He is not like someone that sees from a tower that someone is going to be killed by another, but cannot come in time to help, or that sees a boat shipwrecked on the shore but cannot run to assist it. By this meaning, another Hebrew word is in conformity with the name of God, namely, Eloim, that is judge, because God does not see everything like an idle spectator, but as a judge who examines, discerns, proves and disproves all things, and punishes the wicked while rewarding the good; thus, he is present in all things. Yet, because we do not easily comprehend how God is altogether everywhere, therefore, we say that he runs very quickly, to be present everywhere immediately. Hence the Scripture, "His word runs quickly,"[11] that is his command. For God to act, he does not need instruments or hands, but only a word. "He spoke and they were made;"[12] "Wisdom is more agile than all agile things,"[13] *i.e.* he surpasses all in speed. And this is proper to God, he runs so quickly that he overtakes every event.

Not only does God see all things and is present to all, but he can also impede or promote all things most efficaciously. For we often foresee threatening evils, and are quickly present, but we do not avail to resist. But God can resist everything and no man can resist him. Therefore,

---

[11] Psalm 147:15.
[12] Psalm 32:9.
[13] Wisdom 7:24.

he is said to burn because we have nothing more efficacious than fire. For that reason, Scripture also says: "Our God is a consuming fire."[14] And three Hebrew names are in conformity: *adonai*, i.e. Lord, *el*, i.e. strong, and *sadai*, i.e. most sufficient to all things. And this is also proper to God alone, namely, that he can do all things as the proper and absolute master of all things.

Therefore, we have from the names of God that God knows all things, is everywhere, and can do all things. But there is another name of God, unknown to the Greeks, that was revealed by God to Moses, his most dear servant, which is called "ineffable", but more recent authors call it, *Jeova*. This name means that God is the source of everything. God is himself comprehending whatever is good in all affairs, and in an infinite number of created things. Moreover, it appears how great the happiness of the friends of God is, who have a friend who always sees them, even when they sleep, and runs to them as quickly as he can to defend them from all evil; and besides, he contains in himself and is readily available to communicate all goods to them. How vain and foolish men run and labor, in order to discover imperfect goods when they can have all things in God; life, light, beauty, sweetness, riches, honors, rest, etc.

Another way to discover God is through creation. For created things are pressed in the footprints of their creator, and certain creatures are images of the creator. This is why the Apostle

---

[14] Deut. 4:24.

First Sermon on the Annunciation

says: "The invisible things of God are seen, understood by the things that were made."[15] Think of the magnitude of the earth with all the things that are in it; metals, plants, animals, the waters with all fish, the air with all the birds, the heavens with all the stars; and besides all men with all their wisdom, power and glory, and then add all the Angels who, just as they are in a higher place, so they surpass men in number, wisdom, power and glory.

All these things, which are said under the one word of *world*, have not always existed. For Scripture says that before six thousand years there was nothing, and the same thing is clear from the histories of all nations. For no memory of anything earlier exists in the history of nations, not even in Bellus and Ninus,[16] which existed in the times of Abraham. Therefore, all these things were made, they did not make themselves, because they can do nothing by themselves. What makes ought to exist, what is made, ought not to exist; therefore, they were made by another, who was not made, but always existed. We call that God, who necessarily has these conditions: 1) that he always existed, otherwise we would ask who made him; 2) that he preserves whatever is good in the whole world by his strength, for no man gives what he does not have; 3) that he would be far better than the whole world, because an equivocal cause is better

---

[15] Romans 1:20.

[16] Bellus and Ninus are respectively Nimrod, the nephew of Cham, and Assur the founder of Niniveh. –Translator's note.

than an effect; 4) that he is the infinite good, the font of every good, depending upon nothing, for which reason all things depend upon him. And this, as we said, signifies the ineffable name of God.

Now let us see what Scripture says. "For you made heaven and earth, and whatever is contained in the world's embrace."[17] It also says: "You are the Lord of all things."[18] "There is not one who can resist your will."[19] "There is no end of his magnitude."[20] "Of his wisdom there is no number."[21] There are others of this sort. But I wish to explain one passage, that of Isaiah 40:12: "Who has measured the waters in the hollow of his hand, and weighed the heavens with his palm? Who has weighed out with three fingers the bulk of the earth?" If someone could contain all the seas, lakes and rivers in the palm of his hand, who would be equal to the immensity of the heavens with one palm, who, wishing to know the weight of the whole earth, could hold it up with three fingers: how great he would be! But God does not do this with the mass of the body, but with power. This is a small thing; therefore, the Prophet adds: "Behold the gentiles as a drop of liquid, and are measured on the scale as a balance."[22] What is more scanty, insignificant or fragile than a drop of liquid, which falls with

---

[17] Esther 13:10.
[18] 2 Mach. 14:35.
[19] Esther 13:9.
[20] Psalm 144:3.
[21] Psalm 146:5.
[22] Isaiah 40:15.

scarcely any impact and perishes? But by a lesser impact still the balance of the scale is moved. When the scale is in equilibrium, a little wind suffices to make it move. Therefore, to this smallest of matters, and so easily moveable, all wisdom and power of all nations is compared in respect to God.

But still he has said little, therefore, he adds: "All nations are before him as if they had no being at all, and are counted to him as nothing, and vanity;"[23] *i.e.*, not only all nations with all their power and wisdom are nothing, but plainly of no importance in the sight of God. God will not labor more to resist the whole world, if it should rise against him, than he would ro resist nothing and emptiness. These things are not said to diminish creation. Truly the earth is great and massive, the great breadth of the sea, the great height of heaven, the incredible diversity of plants, animals, stars, the incredible power of the sea, fire, the winds; the great beauty of the stars; the greatest genius of men, the greatest wisdom of the Angels. And still, the excellence of God is so great, that all these are clearly nothing in his sight, just as Job says: "The stars are not pure in his sight,"[24] and they certainly are very pure and lucid, but in the presence of the inaccessible light, they seem impure and dark.

Behold how great he is, who sends the legation to the earth for peace, for friendship, to contract affinity with us. Why do this? Who

---

[23] Isaiah 40:17.
[24] Job 25:5.

moved God to this? Was he afraid we would harm him? But he is almighty. Did he fear that we would surpass him in astuteness? But he is the most wise. Did he need our works? He does not need our works. Perhaps, would he harm us? Rather, we have offended him. Would we ask him or another on our behalf? But we did not even think of it. So why? Pure charity moved him, which is without end, and the abundance of mercy which moved him, to create us when we did not exist, also moved him to restore us, and restore us in this stupendous manner.

This is why we ought to learn: 1) that we must love such a lover in return; 2) that we must imitate him and exercise that pure love toward our neighbor. Who, that regard himself as insignificant, will not be the first to seek peace from his enemies if God did this very thing? And especially in this time, in which we call to mind this kindness of God, etc.

Second Sermon on the text, Missus est Angelus

Given on the Second Sunday of Advent
10 December 1610

E must speak about the messenger, who is the Angel Gabriel, but first on the excellence of the angels in general, which will be useful: 1) to learn the magnitude of this legation; 2) to learn what a blessing from God our guardian Angel is; 3) because in today's Gospel, John the Baptist is called an Angel: "Behold, I send my angel,"[25] and Christ himself is called "Angel of great counsel" by Isaiah.[26] For that reason, from the knowledge of the angelic excellence, we shall know the excellence of Christ's precursor, and of Christ himself, but by one and another manner. That of the great precursor is known because he was similar to the fathers, but that of Christ, because he is so much greater than the great.

Therefore, angels are, by their spiritual natures, a medium between God and man. "You reduced him a little more than the angels,"[27] that is, human nature is a little lower than the angelic nature. The reason is that Angels are perfect spiritual natures, and they do not need a body for their operations. Human nature has one spiritual

---

[25] Matthew 11:2-10.
[26] Isaiah 9:6, in the Septuagint.
[27] Ps. 8:6.

part, but imperfect, and therefore needs another part. So man is part angel, part beast; part gold, part dirt; an angel is all gold. Angels are many in number, in a higher place, created first, beatified first, more powerful, wiser, and naturally better than men. For that reason, St. Ambrose calls them the flowers of all things.[28] But from the corporal picture we understand something of their properties. Angels are painted, not because they have bodies themselves, but because they usually appear that way in a body taken from the air, and to express their nature through similitudes, in the way that virtues are painted.

Therefore, they are painted as beautiful young men, with eyes, ears, noses, a mouth, hands, feet, and wings are added, because Scripture says that Seraphim have six wings,[29] Cherubim have four wings,[30] and Daniel says: "Behold, the man Gabriel came to me flying quickly."[31] And Moses and Solomon placed upon the ark sculptures of Cherubim with wings. Then, they are painted as girded and clothed with a sacred mantle, with a deacon's stole. They are always painted as youths, so that it be shown that they never grow old, nor change their nature since they are incorruptible; such as the sun and stars are also, as well as our bodies will be after the resurrection. For now we are daily changed, etc. They are painted as very beautiful to show

---

[28] Ambrose, *in Luc.* VII, n. 126, coll. VIII, n. 29; ML 15, 1751, 1774.
[29] Isaiah 6:2.
[30] 3 Kings 6:27.
[31] Daniel 9:21.

their internal beauty or, just as bodies are beautiful which have all the members, whole, proportionate, with a sweet color, so spirits are beautiful when they have all justice, which is a certain marvelous proportion of all virtues, and the light of wisdom, which is in place of color.

For that reason God is of infinite beauty, because he is justice itself and infinite wisdom, and it is impossible to see God and not immediately be taken into his most burning love. The holy angels are all very beautiful because they are most just, since they never sinned nor could ever sin, and they are rightly ordered toward God, the other angels, men, etc., and because they are most wise, since they see the first cause of all things.

They are painted with their eyes always open because they never sleep, but are always awake, both contemplating the face of God and safeguarding the men consigned to them. Christ speaks on the fact that the angels are guardians of individual men, "Do not despise one of these little ones, because their angels always see the face of the Father."[32] It is a great benefit, as if a great prince were given by a King as a slave to some poor school child. "It is his Angel."[33] Our ingratitude is great, because we so rarely remember the angels who are always waking to guard us. They are painted with ears, because they are always intent "to hear the sound of the words of God," as the Psalmist says.[34] Likewise,

---

[32] Matthew 18:10.
[33] Acts 12:15.
[34] Psalm 102:20.

because they always hear our prayers, and relate them to God, "I offered your prayer to the Lord."[35] They are said to carry our prayers, because they assist them with their intercession, that they might reach God, *i.e.* that they might be heard, just as nobles assist the supplications of the poor with the king. They are painted with noses, because they thus distinguish best the vices from the virtues. For the nose is the sense of discretion. Often rotting matter, which is not distinguished by sight or touch, is immediately distinguished by the smell, for which reason a man is said to have a good nose who is refined in judgment and discretion. Men often fail in judging works and persons, because they do not see anything but what *is on the outside.* But the holy angels cannot be deceived. They immediately sense the odor of virtue and the stench of sin. They are painted with a mouth because they speak and eat and drink. "If I speak with the tongues of men and angels,"[36] St. Paul says; and in Tobit we read, "I take invisible food and drink."[37] The angels speak, they praise God, they sing, etc., but they do not need a tongue, nor air, nor syllables, for in a moment they mean that which they will. Moreover, they eat and drink wisdom. This is the food of spirits, "He ate it with the bread of life and understanding, and he drank it with the water of salutary wisdom."[38] For us bread, wine, meat, and water are all different

---

[35] Tobit 12:12.
[36] 1 Cor. 13:1.
[37] Tobit 12:19.
[38] Eccli. 15:3.

things, but for the angels it is wholly wisdom, because in as much as the matter is higher, so much more does it sustain. So to God everything is one, that is, his essence is for him food, drink, clothing, house, riches, etc. The angels need more, but much less than we do, etc., and that food is very sweet and continuous, nor does it beget nausea or disgust, etc. They are painted with arms and hands, because they are very powerful in work. "Powerful by strength," the Psalmist says.[39] Power is discerned 1) in bodies which they assume. For to compress the air, to form, to make a shape, to paint, that altogether they would not be distinguished from other living human bodies, takes the greatest power. It is certain that bodies were assumed by the angels that appeared to Abraham, Lot, Tobit and others, that could not be distinguished from humans; 2) In the very speedy embrace of men, such as when an angel carried Habakkuk into Babylon, Elijah into heaven, etc.; 3) In the slaughter of men, as when one angel slaughtered 185,000 men in the army of Senacherib on the spot, and another slew all the firstborn of Egypt.[40]

They are painted with wings because they move very quickly. Nothing that moves so quickly is corporal, neither stars nor winds nor lightning. For without a medium they go across from one place to another, as Gregory of Nyssa writes, as well as St. Thomas.[41] For that reason,

---

[39] 102:20.
[40] Exodus 12:29.
[41] Greg. Nyss., *De anima* I, 11; ed. Basil., 1562, p. 497; Thom. Aqu., *S. Theol.* I q. 53, a 2.

even when a guardian angel is in the highest heaven, by far in a different place from us, yet there is no danger that he would not be present in time, because he clearly sees us and our miseries, and is immediately present because he does not cross the heavens and the air, but comes without a medium. For that reason, on account of their speed, David compares them to the wind, while on account of their power, to fire, "He who makes your angels spirits, and your ministers a burning fire."⁴²

They are painted with naked and clean feet because they are free from every counterfeit and unclean affection, and live among us in the way that light passes through mud and filth yet is not polluted. It is false, which some of the fathers said, that the angels loved women, because it is written in Genesis 6:2, "The sons of God seeing the daughters of men were beautiful, took them to themselves as wives from all that they chose." They love us with a pure love, without any other interest. This is what the white garments mean, in which they usually appear, as is clear from the last chapter of Mark.⁴³ Lastly, they are painted as clothed in a sacred stole so that we would understand they are provided with obedience to God. For there is nothing which they delay from the most prompt obedience. We delay often either from the corruption of nature or from various necessities, in which we must serve the body and the soul, or from temptations. They,

---

⁴² Psalm 103:4.
⁴³ Mark 20:5; Act. 1:10.

however, are free, they have nothing of their own business. And this is what the sacred stole means, that they are sacred ministers, for whatever they do, they do in honor of God.

From these three things we have what we said from the beginning: now, about Gabriel. There are nine orders of angels; for that reason, even in the Church, there are nine ecclesiastical orders, if we number the Episcopacy and the first tonsure. Gabriel is placed by many in the second order, *i.e.* among the Archangels; by others, in the first place, *i.e.* among the Seraphim, because some, such as Dionysius, think they are not sent from the three lowest orders,[44] while some think they are sent from every order. It is certain that Gabriel is a very great Angel, and to him above all others this very great mystery was revealed, for he revealed to Daniel the time of the arrival of the Messiah.[45] He also appeared to Zachariah and announced the birth of the forerunner, and then appeared and announced to Blessed Mary this mystery.

But in what form did he appear to the Virgin? An angel can appear in three ways: in his own essence, in an interior image, and in an exterior image. In the first way, he cannot be seen except in the mind, separated from the body. So we will see them in heaven. In the second way, he is seen in a dream, as is clear from St.

---

[44] Dion. Areop., *de coel.*; Hier. cap. 7, 9, et 13; MG 3, 205, 209, 257, 300-308, coll. *S. Theol.* 1 q. 112, a 2 and Greg. M. *Hom.*, in ep. XXXIV, 12; ML 76 1254.
[45] Daniel 9:20-27.

Joseph: "The angel appeared to Joseph in a dream."⁴⁶ Nor, therefore, must it be believed in every dream. In the third way, he is seen with the eyes of the body, as clearly happened with Abraham and Tobit, etc. It is certain that he appeared to the Blessed Virgin in an exterior image, *i.e.* in human form, but with splendor so that he would be understood to be an angel; in the same way, the three Marys saw angels at another time. 1) The Evangelist says: "The angel came to her." 2) In Greek, verse 29 has: "Who, when she had seen [him], she was disturbed." And in the responsory: *Expavescit Virgo de lumine.*⁴⁷ 3) It was fitting that the Virgin would be very certain about the messenger. Those things are more certain when they are seen by the eyes and heard by the ears, etc. 4) Gabriel appeared in bodily appearance to Daniel and Zachariah, why not to the Virgin? 5) The Fathers say that angels usually appear in human form to honor the nature with which they knew God was going to honor with the supreme honor of the Incarnation; but this was very suitable at that time, in which the Incarnation itself was announced.

Here can be added something from the imitation of angelic purity and obedience, since we are going to be fellow citizens with them.

---

⁴⁶ Matthew 1:20, 2:13.
⁴⁷ *"The Virgin was frightened by the light." Breviarium Romanum*, in festo Ann. BMV, 25 Martius, *ad lect.* primam.

Another sermon Missus est Angelus for the year 1606

Also given on the Second Sunday of Advent
10 December 1606

"In a city of Galilee, named Nazareth, to a virgin betrothed to a man, whose name was Joseph of the house of David, and the name of the Virgin was Mary."

HE Evangelist describes most diligently where the angel was sent to. He was sent, he says, into the province of Galilee, to the city of Nazareth in Galilee, in a certain house, where there was a Virgin; and this Virgin was betrothed to a man by the name of Joseph, etc. God ordinarily chooses low things, as the Apostle says: "God chose the weak and contemptible things of the world."[48] Galilee was a vile and despised province, as it is read in John: "Search the Scriptures, because no prophet rises from Galilee."[49] From that place there are no Princes, no Prophets, and no great men. Nazareth was also a vile city in that province, for which reason Nathanael says: "Can anything good be from Nazareth?"[50] The house of the Virgin was a poor hovel, as can be seen even today. The Virgin herself, although from royal

---
[48] 1 Cor. 1:28.
[49] John 7:52.
[50] John 1:46.

progeny, nevertheless was reduced to marrying a carpenter.

Why is this? 1) That she might teach us humility and contempt of those things that are lofty in the eyes of men, that, freed from the love of visible things, as if after a certain veil has been lifted from the eyes, we would understand and desire invisible things which are true and eternal goods; 2) that she might show her virtue, "for the virtue of God is perfected in weakness."[51] If the instruments were most suitable, a share of glory might be given to the instruments; but now the whole is of God; 3) That the greatest mystery would be hidden from the proud and the wise in their own eyes and revealed to children. The proud Pharisees, knowing the Messiah was going to come from Bethlehem, according to the prophecy of Micah (5:2), after hearing that Christ is a Galilean and Nazarene, because they thought they were wise, did not deign to seek any further, and so remained infidels: but the humble, desiring to learn, knew that he was born in Bethlehem, etc. "I confess to you Father, because you have hidden these from the wise and prudent, and revealed them to these little ones,"[52] and, "I have not come in judgment against this world, but that they who do not see shall see, and those who see will become blind."[53]

But, although God may choose lowly things, still, he does not leave them in a low place, but exalts them. See how he exalted the name of the

---

[51] Matthew 11:25 and Luke 10:21.
[52] Matthew 11:25.
[53] John 9:39.

country, as Our Lord, appearing glorious from heaven, had said: "I am Jesus the Nazarene, whom you are persecuting."[54] Although he did not save the little house, he transferred it by the hands of Angels, and rendered it honorable over the whole world, when the palace of Solomon, Herod, Nero and other similar ones lay overturned in ruins. About the Virgin, what will we say: from the spouse of a carpenter, she became the mother of God, the queen of the world? Therefore, those who are wisely ambitious, let them know the true way is humility.

"To a virgin betrothed to a man." The Angel is very rightly sent to a Virgin, because virginity is an angelic virtue; and especially to the Virgin Mary, who was a terrestrial angel, without any stain of sin, full of wisdom and grace, the heavenly angel is sent. God willed his mother to be a virgin and betrothed, nay more, even married: 1) that he might hide the mystery, for it ought, in an agreeable time and manner, to be made manifest by a forerunner; 2) That he might provide for her honor lest fornication would be supposed; 3) to have a witness for her purity and a helper in her journeys and labors; 4) to approve the state of virgins as well as continence and marriage. He only condemned the state of concubines and courtesans, against the heretics who condemn either marriage or continence. Still, she ought to have been a virgin, and a perpetual virgin, and dedicated to God by vow,

---

[54] Acts 22:8.

because it would not be fitting for the Holy of Holies to be born except from the highest degree of sanctity. Such are virgins to God when obliged by a vow, because they "think of those things which are of the Lord, that they might be holy in body and in spirit."[55]

"Whose name was Joseph." St. Joseph, without a doubt, is one of the greatest men, and that he was divinely chosen as the spouse of the Blessed Virgin is reason enough to believe this. For this marriage was altogether made by God, and, moreover, in the best way in which it ought to be done. For when marriages are well made, the bridegroom and bride are equal or nearly equal, that one might be worthy of the other. But if Joseph was a worthy spouse of the Blessed Virgin, think how great his perfection must have been. Without a doubt he was most faithful, most chaste, and prudent. Further, it is added: "from the house of David," that we might know that Christ descended from David according to the prophecies, not only on the side of his true and natural mother, but also from the side of his putative father.

When the Evangelist uses the proper name, he shows that his etymology must be known. For in the Old Testament, names full of mystery were given, especially those which were given by God. Joseph means *rising*, and is fulfilled in Joseph the patriarch, because he alone among all the sons of Jacob made two tribes, Ephraim and Manasseh, the others only one. The meaning of his name is

---

[55] 1 Cor. 7:34.

also fulfilled in our Joseph. For the greatness of the house of David had always diminished, even to Joseph; but in him it began to rise, and it rose even to the highest heaven, when he had as a wife the queen of heaven, and would be called the father of God.

"And the name of the Virgin was Mary." The name of the Virgin, without a doubt, was divinely imposed, as was the name of John and many others. For it means in Hebrew, a drop of the sea. For *Mar* means drop of liquid, *iam* the sea; hence *Mariam* is a drop of the sea. It can also mean star, or light of the sea, because *Maor* means a lamp. Therefore, this name means the lofty humility of the Virgin and exaltation. In their eyes there was nothing more worthless than a drop of liquid. And if the sea is the human race, a drop of that sea is the most common and least particle of the human race; but in the eyes of God, it was a great light and so was exalted even to the heaven, that it might be greater, more sublime, more lucid than the whole sea, and all the great sailors look upon her, that they might arrive at the port.

"And the Angel, approaching her, said." The angels can be seen in three ways. In their substance, in their interior image, and in the body they have taken up. In the first way they are seen only in the intellect; in the second way by imagination in dreams; in the third way by the corporal eye. In the first way they are seen only in their heavenly country. And this is our great misery, because they are our countrymen and friends, nay more, even servants, but we cannot see them exactly as they are. In the second way

St. Joseph saw: "The angel appeared to Joseph in a dream."[56] Many others also saw them, but it must not be believed to be the case in every dream. See Sirach 34:1-7, and St. Gregory in the *Dialogue*,[57] where he posits the example of a certain observer of dreams, who dreamt that he was going to have the longest life, and therefore became very eager to accumulate money, but immediately he died leaving it all behind. In the third way many also see them, such as Abraham, Lot, Tobit, Daniel, the shepherds, the three Marys, and others. And this is a wonderful power and wisdom of the angels, because they so form and fashion their bodies from the air, that they altogether seem to be men. In this third way the Blessed Virgin saw him; for this is what it means when it says: "He approached," viz. through the door in human fashion, and that verse: "Who, when she saw," as it is held in the Greek text, or, "when she heard," as it is in the Latin. For both are true, and from both a corporal apparition is gathered. And besides, the Virgin ought to be very certain on this mystery. Things that are seen are more certain than those that are only known in the imagination. The Fathers write that the angels usually assume human form to honor that nature which they knew God was going to honor by the incarnation. Consequently, now it was exceedingly fitting that the Angel Gabriel appear in human form, when he was going to announce the Incarnation itself. Lastly, the same Gabriel

---

[56] Matthew 1:20.
[57] Greg. M., *Dial.* IV, 48-49; ML 77, 410-411.

appeared visibly to Daniel and Zachariah, why not to the Blessed Virgin?

Therefore the approaching angel firstly gave greetings, saying: "Hail, full of grace, the Lord is with you. Blessed are you among women." That *hail (ave)* could also be rendered into Greek as "*rejoice*",[58] and the sense would be good because, without a doubt, he announced a great joy to her; but nevertheless, it is rendered better as *hail*, that it might be a salutation. For the Evangelist says a little after: "She wondered what kind of greeting this might be." Then he greeted her with a great announcement: "*full of grace*," and again, repeats: "*the Lord is with you*," with another announcement: "Blessed are you among women."

When he says "*hail*," (*ave*) it must not be understood that he desired to greet her as if there was a danger that she would not be well, for we also say to God: "Health to our God."[59] But this salutation expresses joy about health if it is present, and a good desire that it mightbe preserved if present, and given if it is not. For it is a sign of friendship. This is why greetings are not made to the excommunicated, because we refuse friendship or conversation with them.

---

[58] Latin *ave*, Greek: χαῖρε [chaire].

[59] Apoc. 7:10. This entire discourse will be lost in English because we do not have the common greeting of "health" that is seen in Latin and many other languages. *Ave* comes from *salve*, which means health, and the word *salus, salutis*, means health, but doubles as salvation, thus eternal salvation is *eternal health*. -Translator's note.

Full of Grace. There are three effects of grace: 1) to abolish sins; 2) to make the soul beautiful and thankful to God; 3) to give the strength to do good things and works of prayer that they may become worthy of the reward of eternal life, for example, like what alchemy purports to do, to turn bronze into gold. In all things the Blessed Virgin excelled, therefore she was most thankful, as it is held in the Greek,[60] and full of grace, as it is in Latin, and it is the same sense. In the first effect there are many degrees, for one is to blot out a sin that has been committed, the other is a higher grace that comes earlier lest it should be committed. Likewise, one is to blot out or prevent a mortal sin, another, to blot out or prevent venial sins. The one prevents something, the other prevents everything. In some saints the grace present was penance, blotting out the sins that had been committed, such as in Peter, Paul and the Magdalene; in others, it is the grace of innocence preventing mortal sins, such as in Jeremiah, John the Baptist, and others: but in no one apart from the Blessed Virgin was grace forestalling all sins. And therefore, she was full of grace, for which reason it is said truly from that verse: "*Tota pulchra es, et macula non est in te.*"[61] The second effect of grace is to add beauty. For this reason, grace does not wash stains, in the way of simple water, but as scented water, etc., or it repairs tears not with a simple string, but with gold. The Blessed Virgin

---

[60] Greek: κεχαριτωμένη [kecharitōmenē].

[61] Cant. 4:7. You are all beautiful and there is no stain in you.

was full of all virtues and gifts, etc. In the third effect there is also a step, for some make many meritorious works, others fewer, some lesser, some greater. The Blessed Virgin was excellent in all these, because all her works were meritorious, and that in the highest degree, because they arose from the greatest charity, as is clear from the reward.

But one might say, Elizabeth is said to have been "filled with the Holy Spirit," and likewise Zachary.[62] Stephen is said to be full of grace.[63] So it is, but they are called full of grace with respect to their office, but not simply; that is Zachariah and Elizabeth were filled with the Holy Spirit, meaning they had the grace of the Holy Spirit sufficient to know and give witness to the mystery of the incarnation. The Apostles were full in order to preach in different languages, do miracles, and convert the world. Stephen was full in order to receive martyrdom the first of all. They were all full, and still the grace was unequal, because the vessels were unequal. But the Blessed Virgin was full according to the supreme office that she would be the mother of God, the queen of all saints and angels, and therefore had a greater capacity, and therefore was full of grace more than the rest.

The Lord is with you. This is another announcement, in which she is declared the font and origin of every grace that is going to be given. From where do all these things arise? From

---

[62] Luke 1:41; 67.
[63] Acts 2:4.

the friendship of God, because God was always near her by a singular benevolence, infusing her with gifts and always preserving her, just in the way a river of water gives fluid to the nearby plants to make them mature and bear fruit and so that their leaves do not fall, as it is related in Psalm 1:3. For truly, Blessed Mary is that tree placed next to the river of flowing water, which always retains its leaves, that is, the honor of virginity, and it bears a singular fruit in her time, and all its works attain maturity.

Blessed are you among women. This is another proclamation though it is more particular, insinuating from afar the glory of the motherhood of God, which, that it might more easily be understood, he prefaced with the fact that she is full of grace. "Blessed among women" means that she was chosen apart from all others to the greatest office of conceiving and bearing the Son of God. Yet, she was clearly not ignorant of these things when she said: "Behold all generations will call me blessed."[64] From this gift it arose that she would lack the two evils which all other women have: pain in childbirth and miscarriage; likewise she would have two goods which all others lack: the fruit of a child while at the same time maintaining the flower of virginity. And then, in the Scriptures, it signifies fertility: "He blessed, and said be fruitful and multiply."[65] The Blessed Virgin was blessed among women, because she was the most fertile

---

[64] Luke 1:48.
[65] Genesis 1:22.

of all, and because she bore a son of infinite virtue, who is the exemplar of infinite sons. And besides, by that she became *mother of all the living*,[66] which, as Epiphanius teaches, was the title of Eve to prefigure Mary.[67]

If anyone would like to be visited by an angel, he ought to be in bed, that is, at some time to collect himself and attend to himself and God, and if he wishes to be filled with grace, he ought to imitate the Virgin, who was most humble and free from every vanity. For the vessel in which grace is received is humility; for God "resists the proud and gives grace to the humble."[68] However much greater the humility, so much more capacity the vessel has. What wonder if we would have little or no grace, when we are so proud? It would behoove us to be hollow, and all would try to be mountains, to ascend high, etc. True humility is a rare bird; grace is also rare. The vessel, if it would not be empty, certainly cannot be filled. Mary was free from all vanity, all love of the world, and therefore, she was full of grace. Who of us does not have a heart full of some vanity? For one it is ambition, another avarice, another lust, another curiosity for garments, another curiosity for vain knowledge, another playing at the dice, and another appetite, etc. What a great foolishness! God offers gold, the way we pour forth clay. God offers perfume the way we pour forth water, and we refuse it. He means to give the most precious things for

---

[66] Genesis 3:20.
[67] Epiphan., *Haer.* 78, 18; MG 42, 728.
[68] James 4:6.

free, and we prefer to buy vile things with great labor, just as all our days we hold onto trifles and do not weep for our sins instead, just as if we were not in exile among enemies, as if death were not around the corner.

Add that vain things fill the heart, but they do not really fill it. For our heart is always restless, and wandering, but not satisfied and hence is not truly filled. But grace truly fills and puts the heart at rest. For what is grace but the friendship of the almighty God, the richest, the most loveable? "Grace is the best to make the heart firm."[69] St. Paul says that there is nothing better than to acquire the friendship of God, which truly fills and firms and puts at rest; it fills the intellect with light, and affects it with peace. This is the water which if one were to drink it, he would not thirst forever after. Would that some would wish to experience how good it is to seek God alone.

---

[69] Hebrews 13:9.

Third Sermon Missus est.

Preached On the Third Sunday of Advent
Around 17 Dec. 1606

E have explained the Angel's greeting, now before we look to the rest, I must answer one question: Why do all preachers begin their sermon with this salutation? The reason seems to be because the word of God, which before was invisible, is made visible and palpable by the fact of the greeting of the Blessed Virgin by the Angel. Therefore, they greet her so that, with her intercession, the word of God will become visible and palpable in their mouths, that they might more easily be understood. Likewise, because the preacher has an angelic office: just as the angel Gabriel was sent to Mary, so the preacher is sent to the Church, *i.e.* to the Christian people, which is the "virgin betrothed to one man," as the Apostle says.[70] Therefore, the preacher greats the Virgin and asks her that, just as the angel's salutation was so efficacious in her that she conceived and bore the Son of God, so with her intercession may the sermon be efficacious, and Christ conceived in the minds of his hearers by good desire, born through good works, and at length, be called Jesus by the adoption of salvation.

---

[70] 2 Cor. 11:2.

"When she heard, she was exceedingly disturbed by his word, and wondered what such a greeting as this might be."[71] St. Ambrose speaks well when he says that the life of the Blessed Virgin suffices to teach all men.[72] We have in those words more virtues than the words themselves. After listening to the angel, Mary was disturbed, *i.e.* she was afraid. For that reason the angel says: "Do not be afraid." But she was afraid: 1) on account of the reverence and splendor of the Angel. For, what some say, that she was afraid because she saw such a beautiful young man entering her bedroom and greeting her so kindly, does not seem probable to me, because the Holy Angel knew well from such a form he could fall under suspicion. Therefore, though he did enter in the form of a young man, still it was with such splendor and majesty that she could not help but know it was an angel. For, although Mary is greater than the angel in what regards election and grace, nevertheless she was lesser in regard to present glory, because she was mortal and not yet among the blessed. Therefore, she was afraid of the arrival of a blessed and glorious angel. For that reason, the Church also says: "The Virgin became frightened from the light."[73] And everyone is usually afraid at the coming of an angel, as is clear from Daniel, the three Marys, the shepherds, and others. 2) She was afraid on account of zeal for virginity, not

---

[71] Luke 1:28.
[72] *De Virginibus*, II3: ML 16, 223.
[73] *Breviarium Romanum*, in festo Annuntionis B.M.V., 25 Mar. resp. ad lect. primam.

because she suspected the angel, but because she heard him say she was blessed among all women, and knew this blessing in Scripture means fertility. God had said to Abraham: "I will bless you, and multiply your seed as the stars of the sky."[74] "I will bless your wife, and will give you a son from her." Likewise about Ishmael: "I will bless him, and I will give him increase and multiply him exceedingly." And on the first men: "He made them male and female, and blessed them and said, 'Be fruitful and multiply.'"[75]

Still, she was not so fearful that she lost steadfastness, for she did nothing and said nothing indecent. Daniel fell on his face as though dead;[76] Tobias and his son fell down likewise when they learned Raphael was not a man, but an angel;[77] the three Marys, as Mark witnesses, after they saw the angel, fled on the spot, "for fear took possession of them."[78] But Mary did not flee, nor fall, but examined the words of the angel within herself with a steadfast mind. Were we to compare Mary with Eve and with Zacharia, we would see her perfect virtue. Eve saw the serpent speaking to her in a human voice and was persuaded not to believe God, and that she was going to be like God; she was neither afraid nor considered, but assented right away. For that reason, for this boldness and levity she was punished, that she would give birth in

---

[74] Genesis 17:20.
[75] Genesis 1:27.
[76] Daniel 8:18.
[77] Tobit 12:22.
[78] Mark 16:8.

pain, often miscarry, and fear her husband as a master. Zachariah is another extreme; he was so oppressed by terror that when the angel promised him a son, which he sought from a sterile wife, in the name of God, he was so disturbed that he could not call to mind that all things are possible with God, an angel cannot lie, and that often elsewhere the sterile and aged gave birth by the power of God; therefore, he broke out in words of incredulity and was punished by being made mute. But Mary fell upon the royal road, and was neither bold nor rash like Eve, nor oppressed with fear like Zachariah; she was as disturbed as was necessary, and retained steadfastness as she ought.

She showed not only reverence and steadfastness, but even prudence. For nothing is more prudent in a doubtful matter than to be silent and think. "Hear silently," the book of Wisdom says,[79] and St. James says: "May every man be quick to hear and slow to speak."[80] She was thinking what this salutation might be, *i.e.* who is speaking to her, to what end he speaks, why at that time, when she was just a girl, why in that place without witnesses, etc. But in the first place her humility is shown, the proper virtue of Christ and His mother. She hears herself praised by the truthful angel, as full of grace and blessed among women, and not only does she not rejoice, but is disturbed. When a just man is

---

[79] Eccli. 32:9
[80] James 1:19.

praised by mouth, he is scourged in heart. And, "Just as gold is proved in the furnace, so is the just man in the mouth of one praising him."[81] For unless a man were perfectly humble, that he should clearly have no pride, then he cannot resist praise, or else he will become puffed up.

There are three degrees of humility: the first is of beginners, to know his own misery and to despise himself. The second is of those who are proficient, to desire to be known by others and rightly despised. The third is of the perfect, who, although they are truly full of gifts of God, nevertheless place themselves in the last place, and rejoice to be placed after all others, because they do not consider their goods as their own, but as given by the grace of God. Therefore, they do not put themselves first, because they believe if others have these gifts, they are more favored by God. It is like the nature of a tree: as much as it is laden with fruit, so is it more bent to the ground. The Blessed Virgin was in this degree, but she was altogether alone. She was truly full of grace, truly blessed among women, but so much did she not acknowledge this in herself, that she marveled that this was said to her, and was disturbed. There are few in the first degree. For if we were to truly recognize the foulness of sin, we could not suffer ourselves for an hour, and still we do so for years and rejoice, etc. In the second degree there are many fewer; for even if at some time by the witness of conscience we are greedy or gluttonous or lack devotion, etc., still we

---

[81] Proverbs 27:21.

refuse to be held accountable, refuse to be called out; and if someone would say we are angry, and the word is very true, we cannot lay it aside. And if perchance at some time we try to tolerate rebukes and reject praises, if someone were to look inwardly to his heart, he would discover there a greater pride, in which we suffer rebukes lest we seem proud. Why? Because in sacramental confession itself, at some point men gravely accuse themselves, and if the confessor seems to believe and then admonish them, then they try to diminish their sins. Now if there are few in the first degree, and fewer in the second, how many will be in the third? Nearly none. And still, as St. Augustine warns in his work, on *On Holy Virginity*,[82] it is necessary for the measure of humility to be according to the measure of greatness, according to what it says in Wisdom: "As humble as you are in all things, that is how great you are."[83] Otherwise, a learned man, a rich man, a noble constituted in dignity, if he were to lack great humility, would be like a tall house with no foundation, a tree without roots, or a burning candle, which in the very act of giving light benefits others, but only while destroying itself, like water which washes others, and thereby is rendered unclean.

---

[82] *De Sancta Virginitate*, cap. 31. ML 40, 413.
[83] Eccli 3:20.

Then it follows: "And the Angel said to her: 'Do not be afraid, Mary, you have found favor with God. Behold you will conceive a son.'" 1) The Angel gives comfort to the Virgin; 2) He explains the message to her. Therefore, when he says: "Lest you might fear, Mary," he not only said, but even did. For the angels have the good virtue of comfort. This is why when Daniel fell half-dead, and his nerves dissolved from exceeding terror, so that he could not even move a finger, the angel Gabriel said: "Do not fear Daniel,"[84] and he stood aright. St. Athanasius writes in his *Life of St. Anthony*, from the doctrine of the same Anthony, this is the distinction between good and bad angels: that the former can both terrify and comfort, but the latter can only terrify, even if in the beginning they produce joy, etc.[85]

"You have found favor with God." In other words, "lest you marvel because I said you are full of grace, I did not speak so as to deceive you as if attributing this to your merits; rather, I said so because you have all these from God, and since these are so, you need not fear anything since you are the most favored by the Almighty." It must be known, that something is discovered in three ways: 1) By accident, as when someone discovers a treasure which he was not looking for; 2) from intention, as when a trader seeking good pearls discovers one very precious one, or a shepherd discovers a lost sheep sought with great

---

[84] Daniel 10:19.
[85] St. Athanasius, *Vita S. Antonii* 36-37; MG 26, 896-897.

labor; 3) by a middle way, partly by accident, partly by intention, such as when a servant did not intend to be exalted by his master, but, content with his pay intends to serve as diligently as possible; from there, however, it happens that the master, seeing his diligence and prudence, exalts him to greater degrees. This one, as if by accident, discovered that greater degree, because he was not thinking about it, yet did so in some way by intention, because he intended the means which lead to that end. And this is the best kind of soliciting, for even the heathen author said: "Solicit virtues, not supporters."[86]

In the first mode, the grace of eternal election is discovered, for it is called the *lot* by St. Paul, "Who made us worthy to share in the lot of the saints in light."[87] And, "In which we are called predestined by lot, according to what he has proposed, who did all things according to the counsel of his will."[88] For the first grace of vocation is given to those who are not seeking it; we are preceded in that by God, since he loved us first: "I was found by those not looking for me; openly I appeared to those who did not ask me."[89] And in this kind of grace the Blessed Virgin was outstanding, for she found a grace which she was not seeking, because she was not only chosen before the constitution of the world for the highest glory, but it was prepared for her in the

---

[86] Plautus, *Amphitr.* 78.
[87] Colossians 1:12.
[88] Ephesians 1:11.
[89] Romans 10:20.

very creation of her soul, and she was infused with the greatest grace, etc.

In the second mode an increase of grace is found, and eternal life. For this ought to be sought: "Seek first the kingdom of God, and His justice, and all these shall be added to you,"[90] and "He who seeks, finds."[91] Not only should this grace be sought, but one must run after it and fight for it. "He will not be crowned unless he will fight legitimately."[92] "So run, that you might overcome."[93] And in this manner the Blessed Virgin found the grace that she sought, because she pined for nothing else but to increase in the love of God, and to always obtain it more and more.

In the third way she properly found grace with God, for the Blessed Virgin did not intend to be made the Mother of God, nor the Queen of Angels, nay more; she judged herself most unworthy of such a grace, and still she lived so perfectly, that she rendered herself worthy of so great an honor. For the Church says: "That she merited to be made a worthy habitation for your Son,"[94] and St. Ambrose says that she who was chosen for such an office, added to its dignity.[95] So also a great many saints did not intend to have the gift of prophecy or health, or revelations, nor be made Bishops or Popes; still, while they

---

[90] Matthew 6:33.
[91] Matthew 7:8.
[92] 2 Timothy 2:5.
[93] 1 Cor. 9:24.
[94] Collect following the Salve Regina in the Breviary.
[95] *De off.*, I 18, 69; ML 16, 48.

labored to live perfectly and be very humble, they attained to those graces given gratuitously.

Yet, we must especially labor that we might find grace in the second mode. For that which truly makes one good and blessed, we can also seek and acquire with the help of God. This is what the parable on the tradesman seeking good pearls means.[96] The prudent tradesman does not remain at home, nor buys the things that they bring to the door, for he knows only certain cheap things are brought there, which remain from the market: pot herbs, fish, old garments, etc. Precious things are not brought to the door, but remain hidden in workshops of far off regions.

They who remain at home and buy what is conveyed before the door, are those who desire what comes across through the senses, that is temporal goods, and in these they waste their money. And what are these things but cheap and rancid things, left over from others who used them before and later left them behind? But good tradesmen go out from the house of the senses, and wander in mind, even above the heavens, and seek truly precious things. Paul so speaks: "We do not contemplate those things which are seen," viz. with the eyes of the body, "But which are not seen. For those which are seen are temporal, those which are not are eternal."[97] And what are these things? One pearl of great price, *i.e.* the friendship of God, in which all goods are

---

[96] Matthew 13:45.
[97] 2 Cor. 4:18.

contained. This is that *one*, of which the Lord says: "But one thing is necessary."⁹⁸ But after this has been found, it is necessary to sell all things and buy it, *i.e.* to neglect all things, so that this may be held and possessed, etc.

"Behold, you will conceive and bear a son, and you will call him Jesus. He will be great." This is now the very legation in which the son is declared to be born from her, who is going to be the Savior of the people, and the King of the same people forever. This is the whole legation, which we will delve into more diligently in a moment. Now, we must say something briefly on the first words.

Why was it necessary to distinguish the conception so minutely, as well as conception *in utero*, birth, and the name? Wouldn't it have sufficed to say you will have a son? The Holy Spirit willed to confute heretics in particular through the angel and the evangelist before they arose. The demon had once thrust the human race upon destruction by envy; then, after the birth and suffering of Christ he saw that God applied such a remedy that men could ascend to greater glory, so he tried to persuade men through many heresiarchs that Christ was not true God, or true man. For this is the foundation of all salvation. Therefore, God, foreseeing this, clearly taught through John that Christ is the

---

⁹⁸ Luke 10:42.

Eternal Word, true God, through whom all things were made, etc. Through Luke, he clearly teaches that he was conceived as a true man in the woman from the blood of the Virgin, and born through the way of birth just as every other true man, without any pain for the mother, and while preserving the seal of virginity. He foretold to Isaiah: "Behold a Virgin will conceive and bear a son, and his name will be called Emmanuel."[99] The angel uses the same words, but in the second person. Emmanuel and Jesus mean the same thing, for Emmanuel means, "God is with us," *i.e.* the God-man among men. And Jesus could not be absolutely and universally the Savior unless he was God and man, because Christ was not a particular savior, such as Samson, Gideon, Joseph, etc.; rather he was the universal savior, because he was not the savior of one people, but "The Savior of all men,"[100] as the Apostle says, because no man is saved but through him: "There is no other name in which it behooves us to be saved."[101] Likewise, he saves from every evil, not from one or another, like other saviors, such as Joseph from the great famine, etc. For he saves from hell, in which there is a punishment of every kind, and the privation of all goods.

Examine how great is liberation from temporal plagues that threaten the preservation of temporal life, that from there the benefit of Christ might be understood. Lastly, he was a universal savior because he took upon himself all

---

[99] Isaiah 7:14.
[100] 1 Tim. 4:10.
[101] Acts 4:12.

the sins of the world: "Behold the Lamb of God, behold him who takes away the sins of the world," and suffered, as if he had committed all those things.

Therefore, why are all men not saved? Because they refuse to be among the members, for *he is the Savior of his body*, says the Apostle.[102] For this reason it is necessary to grasp the true proposition: prepare for your funeral, and persevere even to the eighth day, that the name of salvation might be imposed. Many never truly grasp it, some grasp it but miscarry, because it is difficult to carry out. Others do not persevere, etc. The parable of the sower in the four corners of the earth teaches the same thing.

---

[102] Ephesians 5:12.

Fourth Sermon Missus est

Given on Christmas Day
25 December 1606

"Behold you will conceive and bear a son."[103]

ODAY we will explain the first part of the Angelic legation, which contains the conception and birth from the Virgin. On the feast of the Circumcision [January 1] we will explain the second part, which is about the name of the infant, and on the last day of the Epiphany, about his kingdom.

Today let us enter in spirit into the cave of the Savior, just as into the holiest temple, nay more just as into heaven full of the choirs of angels. For today has been fulfilled what the Apostle said: "And when he introduced his firstborn into the world he said: 'Let all the angels of God adore him.'"[104] We ought to enter with fear and reverence, saying with the Prophet: "I will enter into your house, I will worship in your holy temple in fear of you."[105] Moreover, constituted there, we will consider the wonders which astound the angels in that infant. They are three: a new body recently formed; a soul resplendent with new splendor; divinity joined by ineffable reasoning to that body and soul.

---

[103] Luke 1:31.
[104] Hebrews 1:6.
[105] Psalm 5:8.

Now to the first: the body of Christ, according to all causes, is new and must be admired, as Jeremiah rightly said, "The Lord created something new upon the earth,"[106] and the Church in prayer: "A new birth by the flesh,"[107] and the Apostle: "Put on the new man."[108] The efficient cause was God alone. God makes other bodies secondary causes, this he made by himself. And the angel means this when he said: "The Holy Spirit will overshadow you." The Virgin asked: How will this happen, that I will conceive when I do not know man? The angel responds: It will not need the work of man, because without a man the Holy Spirit will form the body in your womb.

Moreover, he says "He will overshadow you," not because the Holy Spirit might be moved from place to place, since he is everywhere, "Where will I go away from your Spirit?"[109] But because God is said to come when, by a new effect, he declares his presence. And it is said *he will overshadow,* but not, *he comes,* because he wanted to allude to the mode of visible arrival; for when the Holy Spirit visibly appears, he

---

[106] Jeremiah 31:22.
[107] *Missale Romanum*, Oratio ad tertiam Missam in Nativitate Domini.
[108] Eph. 4:24.
[109] Psalm 138 (139): 7.

always seems to descend from heaven upon men, as is clear from the sight of the dove above Christ, and from the sight of fire over the disciples, just as even "he will overshadow you," was an allusion to the visible arrival *in a bright cloud*.[110]

This work is attributed to the Holy Spirit because it is a work of charity. For otherwise, it was of the whole Trinity, whose outward works are undivided. Still, the Spirit is not the Father of Christ, because he did not generate His body from his substance, but formed it from the customary ground of the craftsman; still, just as some craftsmen contract out common works through students and servants, but only do the outstanding things by themselves, so also God. This is why it is gathered, apart from other bodies, there were some that were most noble and beloved by God, because what God made himself is always better, as everyone says about Adam and Eve and about the wine made by Christ from water, "You have preserved the best wine for last, etc.;"[111] about the eyes of the man born blind; about our bodies after the resurrection, in which there will be no defect. "For God's works are perfect;"[112] "You are more beautiful than the sons of men."[113] And just as all love their own works more than others, so too God; that body was most beloved. This is, therefore, the first novelty, to which others are

---

[110] Matthew 17:5.
[111] John 2:10.
[112] Deut. 32:4.
[113] Psalm 44 (45):3.

connected: that, because God does not need time to do his works, this body was not formed little by little for forty days, but whole in one moment, as St. Basil says.[114] Just as also in birth, without parturition and pain, he came outside the womb straightaway. An example of this can be found in the first herbs and plants, which rose without seed, without sun, without rain, without cultivation of the earth, without the space of time, by the command of God.

This is why the second novelty is on the side of the final cause, for this body was formed to the highest end, that it would be the lodging of a more noble, wiser, and more powerful soul than all the angels; nay more, that it would not only be the temple of divinity, as all just men, but it would be the holy of holies, where the ark and oracle of God properly were; nay more, that it would be the body of God himself, *i.e.* the conjoined instrument, in the way a hand is to us, through which he would work miracles and grace itself, etc. This is why the Apostle says that in Christ, "the fullness of divinity dwelled corporally,"[115] that is, it did not participate in divinity, nor was the divinity there by effect, rather that body truly and properly was united to divinity. So we see how great a body this was. For the house is built based on the greatness of the inhabitant: for the rustic, a cottage; for the craftsman, a lodge; for a citizen, a house; for a

---

[114] Basil, *In S. Christi generat. 4*: MG 31, 1465.
[115] Col. 2:9.

prince, a palace; for a king, a royal house. What is built for God? What house will you build for me? Therefore, the body is most worthy by every sort of honor, whose footprints the Seraphim rejoice to approach, as Cyprian says.[116] Hence it appears how gravely they sin who are either not worthy to receive, or receive unworthily, this body contained in the Sacrament. For these, by the witness of the Apostle, "eat judgment upon themselves,"[117] that is, condemnation.

The third novelty is on the side of matter. This body was made from the purest blood of the immaculate Virgin, which is a singular novelty, which happened neither before nor after. Therefore, Isaiah gives this for the greatest sign: "The Lord himself will give you a sign: behold a Virgin will conceive and bear a son."[118] And the angel, that he might show that now this prophecy has been fulfilled, uses the same words: "Behold, you will conceive and bear a son." And to prove this he uses the example of a sterile and elderly woman, Elizabeth, who had already conceived by the power of God. Now, although it seems a lesser miracle to give conception to a sterile and elderly woman than to a virgin, nevertheless, each is a miracle and each is naturally impossible. Therefore, the angel says: "There will not be any word that is impossible with God." The Jews say the word *virgin* in Hebrew is a word that means a girl, and they

---

[116] Cyprian = Arn., Bonav. *Serm. de Ascensione*, ML 189, 1669.
[117] 1 Cor. 11:29.
[118] Isaiah 7:14.

Fourth Sermon on the Annunciation 135

allege the passage from proverbs, where it is said: "There are three difficulties for me, and the fourth is altogether beyond me: the path of the eagle in the heavens, the path of the serpent upon the earth, the path of a boat in the midst of the sea, and the path of a man in a virgin."[119] But they are blind. What kind of sign would it be for a girl to conceive and give birth, unless she were to remain a virgin? Moreover, that word, ע ל מא [halmah] means a girl, but one kept at home and guarded, as virgin nobles usually are, which is what St. Jerome notes.[120] Furthermore, in the Scripture this word is never received for a woman that has lost her virginity, nay more, in that passage of Proverbs, Solomon does not speak of an impure girl, as the Jews dream up; rather, it is a prophecy of the Lord's birth. For he says it is difficult to find the path by which the eagle flies, and the snake slithers over the rock and the ship in the sea, because they leave no vestige; but it is much more marvelous, and naturally undiscoverable, how a man might pass through a virgin, that is, for a virgin to give birth, and remain truly and properly a virgin.

The fourth novelty is taken on the side of form, which is the complexion and temperament. For the body of Christ was so perfectly mild, that it had no defect and was never sick, even if it suffered a great many labors and kept awake whole nights, and prayed on mountains in the heat of the day. One might say, why did Christ

---

[119] Proverbs 30:18-19.
[120] Hieron., *In Isaiam* lib. III, cap. 7, 14; ML 24, 110.

refuse to suffer illnesses, which are useful for merit? Christ did not suffer illnesses because they either arise from a birth defect, or from a disordered diet; but it was not fitting for God, the author of this body, to be deficient in forming it, nor did it behoove Christ to give up nourishment, etc. The outward sufferings inflicted upon him were enough for patience.

I come now to the soul. God created the soul of Christ in a new mode. For other souls contract original sin as soon as they are created and infused in the body, and thereby contract ignorance, concupiscence, the difficulty to do good, the propensity to evil. For they inherit these things from Adam, because as soon as the soul is infused in a body begotten with carnal concupiscence, that man begins to be a son of Adam, etc. But the soul of Christ had none of this; rather, it was full of grace and wisdom as soon as it was created, as well as having all the virtues, nay more, even essential beatitude, and that grace was in the highest degree because as John the Baptist said: "The Father did not give him a Spirit by measure,"[121] and John the Evangelist said: "We saw him full of grace and truth."[122] He had grace, as the source from which all others might draw: "We all received from his

---

[121] John 3;34.
[122] John 1:16.

fullness."[123] He also had the greatest wisdom, and that from the first. For in him are "all treasures of knowledge and the wisdom of God."[124]

We learn little by little with great difficulty and with errors, as we see from the example of a narrow vase and an oblique mouth, and a full and broad mouth; or the example of a writer and a printer. And then he had beatitude, although he was still passible and mortal. For all gifts were due to Christ as the true Son of God, but he did not receive them except those which were compatible with the office of the Redeemer. This is why he did not receive the qualities of a glorious body, because these would have impeded his passion, his life with men, examples of humility, etc. Nor, on the other hand, did he receive sin or ignorance or concupiscence, because he could abolish the sins of the world. Therefore, he ought to come with the contrary, *i.e.* with innocence and grace, and not with sin or those things which lead to sin, such as ignorance and concupiscence. Consequently, the soul of Christ was from its very creation the most perfect and superior to all the angels.

But the third mystery, *i.e.* the union of soul and body to the person of the Word, is the most sublime of all. For it is not difficult to understand that almighty God formed the human body

---

[123] John 1:14.
[124] Col. 2:3.

without the help of secondary causes, and that he would create the soul full of all gifts; but that the eternal Word, without any change, should unite to itself a human nature in such an unfastenable and tight knot; that a man would begin to truly exist and could be said truly to be the son of a virgin, conceived, born, etc.; this is truly a marvel, out of the ordinary, and has never before happened. Therefore the angel said: "And the power of the most high will overshadow you." For the power of the most high is the Eternal Word, the most sublime Son, about whom it is said: "who carries all things by the word of his strength,"[125] and, "The Lord's arm, to whom is it revealed?"[126] and, "We preach Christ, the power and wisdom of God."[127] Therefore, this power of the most high descended to the Virgin, and in her womb united human nature to himself. And that we might understand that the mode is incomprehensible to us, he is said to have overshadowed her, *i.e.* in the manner that one is covered with a cloud, that we might not marvel if we do not understand. Rather, it will suffice for us to know it happened from this overshadowing that "what will be born from you and sanctified, will be called the Son of God," *i.e.* that the child of Mary will be most holy, and rightly called the Son of God, because he will be the power of the incarnate God. Yet, there is another mystery here. The Son of God is described after the fashion of a cloud overshadowing and covering

---

[125] Hebrews 1:3.
[126] John 12:38.
[127] 1 Cor. 1:24.

the virgin on every side, lest we might think the Son of God was enclosed in the womb of Mary, so that he would be nowhere else, in the way it happens to other infants. For he was inside, as well as outside and everywhere.

But why does John say: "And the word became flesh, and dwelt among us?"[128] So that he might be for us the *way, the truth and the life*, as John himself says:[129] the way for example; the truth for doctrine; the life for merit. And indeed he was the way for an example through thirty years, the truth for doctrine in three years, the life for merit in three hours. For there was a particular merit in the passion on the Cross. From which we understand it is easier to acquire life, which happens immediately through the Sacraments; it is more difficult to be instructed and learn the things necessary to salvation; it is very difficult to pursue and walk the road once it is known. And therefore, to this point, it has been incumbent upon all men, etc. Besides, Christ placed himself in the last and lowest place, *i.e.* in a stable, so that all could imitate him if they wished. For if he had chosen the life of kings or at least of riches, many could not follow him; but a humble and poor life, at least in disposition, all could embrace if they willed. Besides, Christ taught us by this example what amount of temporal and eternal goods must be done; for he received so much less from temporal things than he could; from eternal things he could so much

---

[128] John 1:14.
[129] John 14:6.

more and being poor, at least in affect, all could embrace if they wished, to give respite or to obtain one hour of these goods. O, how badly we imitate our leader and still are made Christ's kin.

[revise]

Fifth Sermon *Missus est Angelus*

Given on the Feast of the Circumcision
1 January 1610

ODAY we begin a new year, and begin in the name of the Lord, because today the name was imposed, "which is above every name."[130] I will speak on the reason why this name merits peculiar reverence, and at the same time will explain the rest of the epistle, which we began on Christmas, because the same epistle is read today.

Therefore, this name *Jesus* is rightly honored with singular reverence: 1) because Paul teaches this when he says, "In the name of Jesus every knee must bend, in heaven, on earth, and hell."[131] Therefore, even if we had no other reason, the authority of Paul would suffice for us, through whom the Holy Spirit spoke; 2) because it is the proper name of our Lord. For all others are common, such as priest, prophet and king, nay more, the name of Christ itself: "Do not touch my Christs;" and the name of God:[132] "I said you are gods;"[133] 3) because it expresses all his benefits, for which reason we are mindful not only of Christ, but even of his benefits, hearing this name. If you were to consider this name in Hebrew, you would have one benefit; if in Greek, you would have another; if you were to consider

---

[130] Philippians 2:9.
[131] Philippians 2:10.
[132] Psalm 104 (105):15.
[133] Psalm 81 (82):6.

the number of letters, another; if the figure whereby it is painted, another. And all these are held in the remaining part of the epistle, in these words: "He that gave himself for us, to redeem us from all iniquity, and cleanse for himself an acceptable people, zealous for good works."[134]

The first benefit is freedom from eternal damnation. Jesus' name in Hebrew means this. For it means "Savior", as is known. And the Angel explained it this way: "You will call his name Jesus, for he will save his people from their sins."[135] The Angel said to the shepherds: "Today a savior is born for you."[136] To save is properly to free from impending death, as when someone is lead to punishment; if anyone would free him, he is said to have saved him. So the Apostles said at sea: "Save us Lord, we are perishing."[137] We all, on account of the sin of Adam, incur three other evils: 1) The punishment of eternal death, "The wages of sin are death;"[138] 2) The interior stain and deformity, "We all became as unclean, and all our justice as the bloody sheets of a woman, and we fall as leaves from the tree, and our iniquity carries us off like the wind."[139] 3) Weakness in doing good works. For, "We are not sufficient to think anything of ourselves,"[140] that is, without the grace of God.

---

[134] Titus 2:14.
[135] Matthew 1:21.
[136] Luke 2:11.
[137] Matthew 8:25.
[138] Romans 6:23.
[139] Isaiah 64:6.
[140] 2 Cor. 3:5.

Salvation most properly pertains to the first and Paul speaks about this when he says: "To redeem us from all iniquity," *i.e.* after the price of his blood was paid to make satisfaction for us, and so prevent us from descending into eternal death to which we had already been condemned. How great is this benefit! Certainly, if we were to ponder it rightly, we would incline with supreme reverence to this name, which represents to us this benefit. Think now how death is eternal, and certainly believe that you were already condemned to it justly and were very near to it, just as near to death as him who now is on the gibbet of the scales; and then you will understand the magnitude of this benefit. Someone that has despaired of doctors, and still by the industry of someone has been healed, how he magnifies this benefit! Nevertheless, if he is freed from death in which he will again fall, he delays death, but he does not evade it. Still, he does the greatest benefit who knows that death is the greatest temporal evil. Then why do we esteem salvation from eternal death as such a small thing? Because we do not understand and hardly believe that it is so. Nevertheless, the Holy Scripture teaches it is; a great many visions also teach it, found in St. Gregory the Great and St. Bede.[141]

The second benefit is gathered from the name of Jesus in Greek. For, as Epiphanius and others hand down,[142] this name, according to the Greek etymology means a doctor. And most truly

---

[141] Greg. M., *Dial*, IV, cap. 52 sqq: ML 77, 413; Bede, *Hist. Eccl.* v. 12: ML 95, 247.
[142] *Adv. hae.* 29, 4: MG 41, 397.

Christ is a doctor, as he said when some murmured, because he lived with sinners: "It is not necessary for the doctor to go to those that are in good health."[143] Not only does Christ save us from future death, but even from present illness. Sin is an illness, if we consider those two evils, stain and weakness. For, the deformity of sin is just like the deformity of the sick man, which has been joined with weakness. And on these, Paul speaks: "And he shall cleanse a people acceptable for himself, a follower of good works."[144] That is, to heal from the plague of sin, and in the way that it makes a beautiful form pale and deformed, and from sick to doing good it makes a strong doer of good works. [revise] Do you wish to see the image of spiritual sickness, *i.e.* of a sinner? Look at one laboring with a burning fever. He throws himself in the bed idle, disfigured by meanness and dryness, so weak that he cannot walk let alone stand. He has lost the taste for all solid foods, and even for wine itself. He only thirsts for water; he thinks, speaks, asks and dreams of nothing else to satiate him. He is truly miserable in this way, since he neglects all delights and only desires the meanest thing, which healthy men hardly deign to look at. Such is a sinner deformed in the sight of God, too weak for good works, without the taste for the good of eternity, and wholly occupied in mean and transitory things, both which cannot satisfy him, and which he cannot refrain, because they

---

[143] Matth. 9:12.
[144] Titus 2:14.

pass by him, just as this life passes by. For that reason, one who is healthy, as Christ was, and John the Baptist, condemn these things, etc. From this plague no one frees us but Christ. The philosophers tried to apply remedies, but nothing obtained its effect, because the plague arises from corrupted nature. Therefore, only the author of nature can abolish it. But when Christ pours fourth his grace, we are immediately healed, cleansed, fortified, we taste good solid things, we scorn transitory waters. And we can not only act well, but cause others to follow good works, *i.e.* professors and agents of good works.

Oh, if Christians would understand their profession. The proper profession of a Christian is not philosophy, medicine, jurisprudence, armies, agriculture, painting, etc. These are common with the Gentiles, with the Jews, and with the heretics. But the proper profession is good works, and just as one might say to a painter: "Make me shoes," and he will respond: "That is not my profession," so a Christian ought to respond to someone persuading him to false testimony, deceit, adultery, etc.: "I do not know, I cannot, it is not my profession, etc." A Roman poet said that some will be sculptors, orators, astrologers, but:

> "Be mindful that you rule the people by right, O Roman.
> "These will be your skills."[145]

---

[145] Vergil, *Aen.* VI, 852.

So it can be said about a Christian: some do whatever they want, they excel in other matters; you, Christian, be mindful to cast off all earthly things. These are your arts: to do good works, and to not turn away from the straight path.

The third benefit is gathered from the number that arises from the letters. For the Hebrew and the Greek have letters in place of a numeric note. From the name of Jesus the number 888 is gathered. This is why, in the first book of the Sibylline verse, the Cumean Sybil, six hundred years before Christ, foretold his coming saying, that the name of the Savior is 888. And on the other hand John wrote in the Apocalypse, that the name of Antichrist is going to be 666.[146] The mystery of these names Bede notes in his Commentary on Luke. The series of 6 in the Scriptures is the number of labor, 7, rest, 8 of beatitude. For that reason Christ suffered on the sixth day, rested on the seventh, and rose on the eighth day in glory. Antichrist has the number of sixes, because the end and fruit of his doctrine is labor and suffering; Christ has a series of eights, because the end and fruit of his doctrine is *the happy hope which we expect*, as Paul says in this epistle. And they are tripled in number to signify a triple dimension. For long labor and suffering will be the lot of the impious in eternity, imposed on them and embracing all evils, and it is deep, *i.e.* pure and solid, without any mixture of goods.

---

[146] For more on this, see *On the Roman Pontiff*, book 3, chapter 10.

The fourth benefit is the greatest of all and gathered from the figure, whereby this name is painted. For it is painted with a cross in the middle to mean the other benefits Christ confers on us by the cross. For this reason, Paul says, "Who gave himself for us."[147] God could free us from hell, by simply pardoning the penalty. He could take care of the plague of sin and give glory merely from the nod of the will. But to show grace and love toward men he willed to give himself and suffer as well as die, and in this way confer those benefits on us. Moreover, he took up the cross from the beginning of his conception, because he knew the jail in which he had been locked up and offered it to the Father for us. Likewise, he knew punishment while in the stable, which he would suffer there, which other infants did not know, and offered himself to the Father for us.

These four benefits ought to be four keys for us, which restrain us, so that we might not again rush into sins, as well as four goads, which incite to good works, etc.

---

[147] Titus 2:14.

Sixth Sermon on Missus est Angelus

Given on the Feast of the Epiphany
6 January 1607

N the words, "He will be great and called Son of the Most High ... and his kingdom will have no end."[148] The last part of the legation remains, which is on the kingdom of the Messiah; and it agrees with the feast of the Epiphany, because today he began to manifest his reign. "Where is he who was born king of the Jews?"[149] And he began to be adored by kings, and because he is not only king of the earth, but also of heaven, therefore, the star from heaven served him like a torch. Furthermore, the angel Gabriel says three things: 1) In general, "He will be great; 2) On his greatness as God, "And he will be called Son of the Most High; 3) on his greatness as man, "And God will give him the throne of David his father, and he will reign over the house of Jacob forever, and his kingdom will have no end."

He will be great. Some are said to be great due to some eminence, such as Alexander the Great, or due to some command, like Pompey the Great on account of his many triumphs, Basil the

---

[148] Matthew 2:2.
[149] Luke 1:32.

Great due to his great doctrine, or Gregory the Great due to his great piety. But Christ is called great in every manner: great power, because he is almighty, great wisdom, etc. Likewise, Alexander was a great king, Pompey a great general, Basil a great teacher, and Gregory a great Pope; but Christ is a great king, great priest, a great prophet and, what excels the rest, the great God. "Looking for the blessed hope and coming of the glory of the great God and our Savior Jesus Christ."[150] For the other gods are either false and thus small, or created—"I have said, you are gods"[151]—and thus, small. For he is the true God and consequently, a great God. "Who is a great God just as our God?"[152]

And then all created things cannot be called great, except in comparison. A mountain is great in regard to the hill, and heaven in respect to the earth; but absolutely nothing created is great, because every created thing is finite, and nothing finite is great. Cicero also knew this, speaking about time, which he denied to be eternal, since it had an end.[153] Only God is absolutely great because, "Of his magnitude there is no end;"[154] "There is no number for his wisdom;"[155] his duration is not limited, etc. "O Israel, how great is

---

[150] Titus 2:13.
[151] Psalm 76 (77): 14.
[152] Psalm 76:14.
[153] Cicero, *De inventione*, I, 26.
[154] Psalm 144 (145): 3.
[155] Psalm 146:5.

Sixth Sermon on the Annunciation

the house of God," Baruch says, and, "the vast place of his possession. It is great and does not have an end, it is lofty and immense."[156] The house of God is eternal and its possession his true essence. This is great without end, the highest on account of infinite excellence of nature, the broadest on account of innumerable perfections, the longest on account of eternal duration. Therefore, Christ was going to be great, because he was the great God and a great man.

And he will be called Son of the Most High. Here his divine greatness is explained in particular, as if he were to say: Not only will he be great, but he will even be recognized as great. For he will be called Son of the Most High God, and by this he will be understood as well as held to be the Son of God. So, we see that in the gospel he is called Son of God by John the Baptist: "No man has ever seen God; his only begotten son, who is in the lap of the Father, He himself will tell you."[157] Later he adds: "I have seen, and born testimony that he is the Son of God."[158] Where he calls him the only begotten, he distinguishes from the sons of God by adoption; and when he says he is in the lap of the Father, he shows that he is

---

[156] Baruch 3:24.
[157] John 1:18.
[158] John 1:34.

of the same nature with the Father. For the Son is said to be in the Father in this way, and the Father in the Son, etc. So later Nathanael, Peter, and Martha said he was the Son of God. Moreover, the demons also affirm this point.[159] Later, the whole world believed and confessed, and on the day of judgment altogether everyone will know him, and, "Every knee will bow," as the Apostle says.[160]

Moreover, the true and natural Son of the Most High, is also necessarily himself the Most High. For as much as there is one nature, so also there is the same highness. And the Pharisees correctly understood this consequent. "They were seeking to kill him, because he said God was his Father, making himself equal to God,"[161] and Paul adds: "Though he was in the form of God, he did not reckon it robbery to be equal with God."[162] Therefore, Christ is also most high because He is the Son of the Most High. Why is he most high? 1) Because by the nobility of his nature he transcends all things; 2) Because he sits over all kings and judges. Those who judge, sit on a lofty throne, and the higher they sit, so much the greater they are. "There is one legislator and judge, who can destroy and save."[163] All other

---

[159] *Cf.* John 10:38; John 1:49; Matthew 14:33 and 16:16; John 6:69; John 11:27; Matthew 8:29.
[160] Philippians 2:6.
[161] John 5:18.
[162] Philippians 2:10.
[163] James 4:12.

Sixth Sermon on the Annunciation

judges have judges over them, and they can be impeded in the execution of the sentence. Only God sits in the highest seat because He judges all and is judged by no one. He can invalidate and impede the sentences of all judges; and He can be impeded by no man, no one can resist him, etc. 3) He is called the most high because he does not sit, except over the highest things of creation. "I dwell in the highest;"[164] "Heaven is my throne."[165] The highest creatures are angels and holy souls that do not think about nor love earthly things. God sits in these, not to rest, but to make them rest in indescribable rest. For God in Himself is quiet and tranquility; although, with certain men he shows himself as a terrible and agitated king, and exercises tremendous judgments condemning to eternal or temporal miseries; with all others he shows himself as a friend, a brother, and a spouse, using incredible familiarity just as kings do when, after putting away their scepter, and leaving behind their throne, they play with their household in the royal chamber.

And the Lord God will give him the throne of David his Father. Here, he relates the greatness of Christ as a man, and says he will be king of Israel just as David his father was. Here we must know that this is not properly understood of the temporal kingdom that David had, since that kingdom was exceedingly small and unworthy of

---

[164] Wisdom 24:7.
[165] Isaiah 66:1.

Christ, as it was over one small province. Thus, Christ would be one of a crowd of little princes. But Scripture says Christ will be king of the whole world. "Ask of me, and I will give to you the nations as your inheritance, and the ends of the earth as your possession."[166] And, "He will rule from sea to sea, and from the river even to the ends of the world. And all the kings will adore him; all nations will serve him."[167] And Isaiah, in that reading which is read today (60:1-6), says, even the kings of the sea and remote islands are going to offer gifts to Christ, and as a sign of this matter today, the kings of foreign nations adore Christ.

Besides, if the angel spoke of David's own kingdom he would have spoken a falsehood because Christ refused that kingdom, even when the crowd meant to choose him. Moreover, *de facto*, Herod held that kingdom while Christ was living, and then Archelaus, then the Romans, then the Saracens, and now the Turks. Therefore, the angel speaks figuratively about the kingdom using the kingdom of David as a model, which in fact is the Church diffused throughout the whole world. For example, it is like a king giving a province and showing it depicted on a document.

Moreover, the kingdom of David was a figure of the kingdom of Christ: 1) because David was anointed king from boyhood, and still only after many labors obtained the kingdom; 2)

---

[166] Psalm 2:8.
[167] Psalm 71 (72):8.

Sixth Sermon on the Annunciation

Because David began his kingdom with poor men, oppressed by foreign debt and a bitter spirit, who still did not roam in the wilderness, as exiles do today, but defended themselves and others, as is clear from the history of Abigail.[168] Then, David always had wars, but his son Solomon supreme peace. So Christ, etc.

And he will reign over the house of Jacob forever, and his kingdom will have no end. The house of Jacob and the kingdom of David are the same. For David ruled over the sons of Jacob. But Scripture changes the names to indicate new mysteries. It is said that Christ will reign over the house of Jacob, although really he ought to reign also over the house of Esau, and over the whole world. For by "Jacob" the elect are understood, by "Esau" the reprobate. "I loved Jacob, but hated Esau."[169] Christ certainly rules the elect, as he also does all the good through the most powerful grace, making them subject to him of their own will, pouring into them fear and charity, etc. Yet, he rules the reprobate and all the wicked with an iron rod, punishing and bridling them, etc. But the prior mode of rule is proper to Christ, consequently, the angel solely calls it to mind. He leaves behind the other mode because it is common to all kings.

He also says: *Over the house of Jacob,* because it was going to be added: *forever.* For the house of Jacob will always be the kingdom of

---

[168] 1 Kings (Samuel) 25.
[169] Romans 9:13.

Christ, whereas the house of Esau will not. For they are said to be of a kingdom who are citizens, and participate in the privileges of the kingdom as well as honors and offices, etc. Captured enemies, however, and those held in prison are not said to be of the kingdom because they do not participate in its goods.

Now, therefore, the good and the bad, the reprobate and the elect, are the kingdom of Christ because all participate in the goods, offices, and dignities of the Church, both laity and ecclesiastics. But on the day of judgment a separation will be made, and all the bad will be cast out from the kingdom of Christ, *i.e.* from the people, from the city, and like enemies cast into the perpetual prisons. And only the house of Jacob will be the kingdom, people, and city of God forever. This is what these verses mean: "The kingdom of God shall be taken from you,"[170] and "... bring my enemies here, and kill them in my sight."[171] The sign that someone is from the house of Jacob is if he does not only have the kingdom of Christ outwardly, but also inwardly maintains the kingdom of God, which is justice, peace and joy in the Holy Spirit.[172]

Now it is easy to acquire a share in the eternal kingdom, later very difficult. An example from the population of the cities, which sold very precious things for a cheap price which they

---

[170] Matth. 21:43.
[171] Luke 19:27.
[172] Romans 14;17.

Sixth Sermon on the Annunciation

could scarcely do at another time. It is a great blindness that labors and sweats for transitory things, and refuses to receive eternal ones for free.

—Finis—

www.ingramcontent.com/pod-product-compliance
Lightning Source LLC
Chambersburg PA
CBHW021445070526
44577CB00002B/264